The Practitioner Inquiry Series

Marilyn Cochran-Smith and Susan L. Lytle, *SERIES EDITORS*

Learning in Small Moments:

Life in an Urban Classroom

Daniel R. Meier

Foreword by Deborah Meier

Teachers College
Columbia University
New York and London

Published by Teachers College Press, 1234 Amsterdam Avenue, New York, NY 10027

Copyright © 1997 by Teachers College, Columbia University

Library of Congress Cataloging-in-Publication Data

Meier, Daniel R.
    Learning in small moments : life in an urban classroom / Daniel R. Meier ; foreword by Deborah Meier.
        p.   cm. — (The practitioner inquiry series)
    ISBN 0-8077-3626-0. — ISBN 0-8077-3627-9
    1. Teaching—United States—Case studies.   2. Teachers—United States—Case studies.   3. Education, Urban—United States—Case studies.   I. Title.   II. Series.
    LB1025.3.M45   1997
    371.1'02—dc21   96-40291

ISBN 0-8077-3626-0 (paper)
ISBN 0-8077-3627-9 (cloth)

Printed on acid-free paper
Manufactured in the United States of America

04 03 02 01 00 99 98 97   8 7 6 5 4 3 2

For my parents–
teachers still

Contents

Foreword

I first encountered Daniel Meier in an odd way. Someone sent me a copy of an article he had written and complimented me on my son's wise and useful voice. I had a son—also a teacher of first graders and also living in California—so it was a natural mistake. And under the circumstances both my son and I were relieved and flattered. We liked what Daniel said and how he said it. It would be all right to be mistaken for relatives.

What makes his voice so valuable to me is its utter directness and honesty about what it feels like and sounds like to work in our most troubled schools. It also tells it as it could take place anywhere. Yet, he tells it as it actually did take place in one particular setting—and to one particular pair of teachers. Directness and honesty may seem to some like trivial traits. But I have read hundreds of books and would-be books, articles and would-be articles, and, in fact, it's rare. We tell our war stories and we tell our stories of perspicacious triumph. But we hesitate to tell what it was really like—the hurt, pain, satisfaction, confusion, and just plain unending hard work. The trial and error that thoughtful and well-educated practitioners have to go through—over and over again—is the untold tale, the "dirty" secret. We are always "new" to teaching. I returned to the classroom after a hiatus of several years—thinking I'd bring to it all my latest wisdom. I flopped, much as Daniel does in the first half of this story. It was a semester-long course, and I never quite recovered. I like to think I would have, had I only had more time.

That grown-ups can be so intimidated, confused, and outwitted by six-year-olds, en masse, always seems to me hard to explain. Unlike Daniel, I kept it a secret when I began teaching. Mostly it's so dreadfully embarrassing, especially since we all know that the children are longing to let us teach well, to be our admirers, to fall in line. They want a good, caring teacher. They want to be properly schooled. So why can't we do it? They test us out, holding back for fear of their own failure, their own defeat. They demand of us a kind of assurance and confidence that we cannot fake and don't always live up to. And all the more so when our styles and signals are alien, confusing, or unnatural to their expectations—when we reach across race, class, and language barriers as Daniel and his colleague do in this classroom.

In its specificities, his love for the children, his respect for their families, his willingness to reexamine old practices, his dogged determination not to let any possibility go unexplored, Daniel is everything we're looking for. He exhibits the qualities that are needed if we are to see to it that our children are all well prepared, all thoughtful citizens and caring neighbors. But it's also clear that Daniel was struggling against some odds that are utterly unnecessary and that the success of the Daniels-to-come will require rethinking both the resources we offer such schools and the ways in which we support teachers like Daniel and John.

I know that every classroom teacher will read this with baited breath, perhaps even with a small knot in the pit of their stomach at times. What will the kids do next? Will it have a happy ending? And as we move through the year with Daniel we recognize scenes, we rethink our own daily experiences, and we come away from it with new insights that can strengthen us for the next year's new class. I think parents, too—regardless of class, race, or social class—will recognize their teachers, their children, and their schools in this account.

Deborah Meier
Founder, Central Park East Schools

Preface

I first learned to teach from a wonderful master teacher. Years later, I still remember her way with the children, the feel of her classroom, the energy of her teaching. And I also remember the "little things"—the way she rolled "all rrright" between words to gain and maintain momentum during a lesson, the way she rang her little bell from the back of the room when the children's noise reached a crescendo.

This book is a portrait of those telling, insightful "little things" that add up to teaching and learning in classrooms. As I describe key scenes and vignettes of the classroom I shared with my co-teacher, John Sierra, I focus in particular on the quality of human relations between children, teachers, and families. As if lifting up a rock with my hands or a stick to see life underneath, I look at the details of movement and size and feel of one urban classroom. In doing so, I draw upon our teaching journals, student work, teaching plan books, and lived memories and recollections of our teaching and learning. For all the children and adults, save John and myself, I use pseudonyms. I have also changed the name of the school.

I tell the story of our year together because teachers, educators, and others are always in need of personal, direct accounts from the classroom. Our particular story is of two teachers from different social and educational backgrounds co-teaching in an urban public school. As told from my perspective as a white male teacher, I describe the intricacies involved in establishing a personal and professional relationship with John, and our common adventure in understanding and improving our shared classroom. I intend the book, also, as a reflective chronicle of the daily, enduring challenges of classroom life. The book, then, is for all those interested in bettering the lives of children and adults in our schools. And I hope readers will see and hear and feel the voices in this story according to their own experiences and hopes and dreams for our children and schools.

In writing the book, I am indebted to our former students, families, and colleagues. Without their support, and our work together, there would be no story to write. I hope that other children and teachers, in other school settings, will benefit from their efforts.

In addition, I am grateful for the enduring and patient appreciation and assistance afforded by my editor, Brian Ellerbeck. He helped me glean a focus for my stories, and helped me believe that these tales from the classroom are worth hearing.

I also wish to thank a number of family and friends who helped shape this book in their own ways—Louise Rosenkrantz, Dan Terris, Robin Larson, Paula Crivello, Ellen Frank, Cathy Barnett, Myron Berkman, Hazelle Fortich, and Andrew, Jeremy, David, and my parents. Their efforts will always be appreciated.

Last, I wish to thank John Sierra, my co-teacher, for his friendship and support in teaching and in writing this book. I appreciate the opportunity he gave me to write about our co-teaching experience with an honest and open voice. Although I have written this book, there would be no story without John, and I hope that John's teaching voice comes through in the telling of our shared classroom.

Daniel R. Meier

Prologue

A recent teacher training exchange program in Mexico allowed me to rediscover how classrooms are microcosms of communities and thus the societies we live in. The time I spent in that Mexican classroom allowed me to see anew how sociological and economic structures within classrooms connect to the larger community and society. What exists in each community, one finds in schools and classrooms serving that community. The difficulty lies in creating opportunities for educators to step back, consider our personal and professional biases, and see the societal structures in our classrooms. As our world is diverse and ever-changing, so are our classrooms. Increasingly, educators realize this and are reflecting upon societal issues of class, race, ethnicity, and gender, which influence the quality of our schools.

When Daniel and I decided to work together, we had little idea how quickly our differences would surface and how our personal and professional friendship would grow from these differences. We were different in education, teaching experiences, religious and family background, and social class. We seemed to represent many of the potentially divisive differences found in American schools.

Not surprisingly, these differences influenced our viewpoints in countless situations we encountered in our shared classroom. Our decisions on how we wanted our students to address us, as Mr. Sierra or as Daniel; how we related as teachers to students, families, and colleagues; our role as teacher/professionals or teacher/community members—all were affected by our histories as individuals and as teachers. Even as fellow graduate students in education, we were not prepared for the complex interaction of class and ethnicity and its influence upon our perspectives in working with the very same group of children. Surely, something similar happens every day in schools across the United States. I feel the pendulum swings from student-centered to teacher-centered, monolingual to multilingual, direct teaching to multiple teaching strategies, are attempts in the educational community to address the multifaceted, complicated human experiences in schools.

What Daniel has done in this book is to bring together what we learned in our year together, and provide teachers and others a scaffold of stories to work from in improving the quality of life in classrooms. When discussing our relations with parents, journal writing, calendar, or math, Daniel shows how teachers can negotiate the diversity of experiences that teachers, children, and families bring into the classroom. To this end, our story as Daniel tells it provides a detailed view of the increasingly complicated life in classrooms.

John Sierra
Roosevelt School District, Phoenix, Arizona

The First Day–
Setting the Tone

My best friend's name is Yasmine.

by Nicole

When I was five years old, I knew the alphabet, I'd been vaccinated (for smallpox), and I could read. So my mother walked across the street to Jefferson Davis Grammar School and asked the principal if she would allow me to enter the first grade after Christmas.

Eudora Welty, *One Writer's Beginnings*

It was the biggest blind date of our lives. Framing the doorway of Room 201, John and I nervously awaited the arrival of our first-grade students and their families. It was to be a day of firsts—the first day of school, our first day co-teaching, our first day teaching at Mayfield School. It was an important day, a day of early impressions and a chance to set the tone for the school year. John and I wanted to make positive connections with our students and their families, and present ourselves as capable teachers and our shared classroom as an exciting place to be.

Charles and his father, Joe, were the first to arrive. Charles strode into the room with a breezy, "Hello, Daniel and John." He easily remembered our names from the previous week's potluck dinner for first-grade families.

Then, in what was quickly becoming a signature gesture, Charles raised his hands in mock disbelief.

"What?" he exclaimed. "No kids? Where is everybody?"

John and I laughed, Charles easing our first-day jitters.

"Don't worry, Charles, they'll be here soon," I said.

As John greeted Joe, I asked Charles to find his name tag on a small table by the doorway. The name tag search was designed to give the children an immediate sense of accomplishment as they entered our classroom. Charles needed no help finding his name. I helped him peel off the plastic backing, and told him to select a cubby. Charles randomly selected a cubby and smacked the tag on the front. He then turned to join John and Joe in conversation— Charles seemed more in the mood for a party than nervous about the first day of school.

Joe said he had to get to work, and gave Charles a bear hug.

"You be good now," he said. "Don't give Daniel and John a hard a time. They seem like nice teachers."

Charles rolled his eyes. "Hey, don't worry. What am I going to do?" he said with a mischievous grin.

I sensed that Charles wanted to chat with us, but with other children arriving, I directed Charles to the tub of Legos on the rug.

2

Like two marionettes moving with perfect synchrony, John and I turned to greet our students and their families.

"Hi," said a tall woman. "I'm Barbara and this is Joey. He's in your class. But I'm not Joey's mother. I'm a neighbor. His mother, Mrs. Brown, works nights and usually can't bring him to school. His older sister will."

We warmly shook hands and welcomed Joey, a tall boy with a ready grin who had already espied the Legos on the rug. After giving Joey the name tag-cubby-activity spiel, he joined Charles.

"This is Antonia," said another woman, "and I'm Mrs. Morgan, Antonia's grandmother. Nice to meet you both. Antonia's mother will normally drop her off."

She placed a gentle hand on Antonia's shoulder.

"Go on. Go on now, sweetheart. It'll be fine. I have to go."

Antonia edged across the doorway, her right thumb and forefinger shyly touching her lips. John sensed Antonia's tentativeness and helped her find her name tag and affix it to a cubby. Antonia moved toward the rug area, slowing at the sight of Joey and Charles's energetic Lego play.

A boy and a teenage girl peeked around the doorway.

"Good morning," John called out. "I'm Mr. Sierra, and what's your name?"

"I'm Jerome," the boy said as he peered up from beneath a silver and black Raiders cap wedged down to his thick, dark eyebrows. "And this is my sister."

Jerome stepped into the classroom and gave his sister a mature, no-look wave over his shoulder.

The 8:45 bell rang outside our classroom, officially ringing in the new school year. Within moments, our doorway became a busy montage of late-arriving students and families. John and I met all the children and, extending hands and smiling, we greeted as many adults as we could. By 9:00, the traffic thinned and we scanned the hallway for any stragglers. Seeing none, we left our doorpost.

John looked to me, and I nodded.

"Boys and girls," John's voiced boomed above the chattering children, the scribbling of crayons, the snapping of Legos.

"It's time to clean up. Please put away your things where you found them and sit in a circle on the rug."

It was our first command, and the troops were obeying.

As John and I sat on wooden chairs on the rug, we faced our class for the first time. Whatever notions the children had for the beginning of first grade, attendance and lunch count were not likely foremost. As so often happens in schools, mostly by force of tradition and habit, paperwork and bureaucracy win out over the more immediately human.

Reversing the last-name, first-name order of our computerized class roster, and in a voice louder and more authoritative than I used in greeting the children moments earlier, I took attendance by reading the children's names. The children didn't question the difference in my voice. Moving from the outside world to the world of school, somehow the children weren't surprised to enter our brand-new relationships as "teachers" and "students."

For lunch count, John and I had read the two-page "Lunch Procedures" sent from the cafeteria, but we suddenly couldn't remember which code (M, L, K) indicated whether children paid full price, reduced, or qualified for a free lunch. John looked on our desk in the back of the room but couldn't find the manual. Like two quarterbacks huddling during a time-out, John and I conferred. But we were still confused; "M, L, K" didn't correspond to the first letter in "Full," "Reduced," or "Free," and when we ran through a list of possible synonyms, the letters still didn't fit. We couldn't ask Belva, our instructional assistant who had taught at Mayfield for many years, because she was downstairs registering new kindergartners.

We finally turned to the children for help.

"Okay," I said calmly, "if you're going to eat in the cafeteria today, please raise your hand."

Up went all 21 hands.

I then realized this wasn't going to work; all the children ate in the cafeteria whether they ate a school or home lunch.

"If you brought your lunch from *home* today, raise your hand."

Up went a few hands. Progress.

"Okay, you can put your hands down now. If you're going to get a *cafeteria* lunch, raise your hand."

Up went a majority of hands.

"Now," I said, gathering momentum, "I'm going to call your name one at a time. When I do, you need to come up and give me your lunch money."

As so often happens in teaching, what begins as an apparently simple instruction quickly proves otherwise. The children produced money from a variety of hiding places—tightly wadded pieces of paper stuck deep in pants pockets, crinkled envelopes, rubber-banded pieces of paper, and backpacks and jackets that required children to traipse to the back of the room and unzip every possible zipper. As the children brought up their money, John and I played banker, organizing and counting the coins and bills. Then, matching each child's amount with the accompanying code, we deduced which children received a full, reduced-price, or free lunch.

In cracking the lunch codes, we had carried out our first joint problem-solving exercise. The entire class worked together to solve the problem, and it had came about by chance, not by our teacherly design.

"You have two teachers this year," I said, making a mini-transition to group introductions. "I'm Mr. Meier and this is Mr. Sierra. You also have another teacher, Mrs. Edgars [Belva], who is our teaching assistant. Mrs. Edgars can't be here today, she's downstairs helping in the office, but she'll be here in the mornings starting tomorrow. Now you can call us Mr. Meier and Mr. Sierra, or if you want, you can call us Daniel and John. Mrs. Edgars wants to be called Mrs. Edgars. I'll be with you half the time, and Mr. Sierra will be with you the other half. One of us will *always* be here with you. There will never be a time when you don't have a teacher. This week we'll both be here every day."

I pointed to our schedule on the bulletin board.

"Starting next week, *Mr. Sierra* will be with you on Mondays and Tuesdays. *I'll* be with you on Wednesdays and Thursdays. On Fridays, Mr. Sierra will teach all day and I'll teach all day the next Friday. So next Friday, Mr. Sierra will be here, and the Friday after that I'll be here."

I paused. The children looked neither puzzled nor as if they understood. Six-year-olds have enough difficulty understanding the very concept of a week, let alone why they have two teachers, whether to call them by their first or last name (or both), and how these teachers will share the teaching schedule. In addition, having a male teacher (not to mention two) was enough of a novelty for the first day of school; by the time most children enter first grade, even if they've been in day care and preschool for three to four years, they have had little or no contact with men in a school setting.

"I know this is a lot to take in all at once, but you'll get the hang of it," I said hopefully. "Now let's play a game. We'll go around the circle saying our names and we'll see if anybody can remember *all* the names at the end."

For one long extended moment, names from the Old and New Testaments, names I'd never heard and had a hard time pronouncing, names from a variety of languages, stretched into one long name above the invisible space of our circle. The children said their names with that special first-day-of-school mix of private and public voices. The beginning of school marked the official end of summer, and the children were now making the time-honored transition from the personal, private world of their homes and communities to the official, public arena of the classroom. Some children, like Warren and Amanda, offered their names with confidence. Others, like Janet and Matthew, looked down shyly as their names bounced off their sneaker tops.

"Every morning when you come in," I said, "we'll sit here in a circle for morning meeting. We'll read the morning message, do the calendar activities, and explain what we're going to do during the day. Now let's look at the morning message."

I stood beside the chalkboard and pointed to the first word in the message. "As I read, try to read along with me."

In my slow, deliberate whole-class reading voice I read the message:

Dear Class,
Good morning!
Welcome to the first day of school.

Amanda and Warren, their voices strong and accurate, kept pace with me as the rest of the class mumbled along.

"Good for you!" I exclaimed. "No one told me you all could read on the first day of school!"

I "passed the baton" to John as I moved to the back of the room.

"Boys and girls," John said with a quick clap of his hands, "look up here at the calendar. Do you see these numbers?"

"Yes," replied the twenty-one-voice chorus.

John pointed to the yellow Day-Glo calendar we had bought at a teacher supply store. We cut out small pictures of five suns and four school buses and placed them in a pattern to represent the first nine days of the month. We numbered the pictures from 1 to 9.

"Let's count these numbers together," John said.

"One, two, three, four, five, six, seven, eight, nine," went the chorus.

"Good. Now here's the tricky part. The nine pictures all make a *pattern*. A pattern is something that gets repeated over and over and over again. Let's say the pattern together as I point to the pictures: sun, school bus, sun, school bus, sun, school bus, sun, school bus, sun. Do you see what gets repeated? Sun–school bus, sun–school bus. That's the basic pattern. Now, who'd like to come up and tell us today's date and the correct picture to continue the pattern?"

John called on Joey, who strode to the front as if he'd just won an Academy Award.

"Yesterday was the ___ ?" John asked as he pointed to the previous day's date.

"Nine."

"Right. The ninth. And so today's date is one more. One more than nine is ___."

"Ten."

"Right. And to keep the pattern going, should it be a sun or a school bus?"

Joey paused. "School bus?"

John nodded and handed Joey a "10" school bus to pin on the calendar.

"Now everybody look down here below the calendar. See these book pockets? These are the days of the week. These three cards say, 'Yesterday, Today, Tomorrow.' Who'd like to come up and put the cards in the right pockets? Careful, this is tricky. 'Tomorrow' needs to go in the 'Tuesday' pocket, 'Today' in the 'Monday' pocket, and 'Yesterday' in the 'Sunday' pocket."

Up went a majority of hands. John called on Amanda, who easily placed the cards.

Maintaining the upbeat tempo and his enthusiasm, John continued, "Look here. On this small piece of blank paper, we'll record the days from the calendar. We're going to use something called tally marks. They help us count and keep track of things."

John wrote four tall vertical lines in black magic marker.

"One, two, three, four. Now, the fifth tally mark goes on the *diagonal*, like this. Then six, seven, eight, nine, and then another diagonal mark. Ten. There are ten tally marks for the ten days of September. Here's one group of five marks and here's another. I'll draw one big circle around both groups to show a group of ten. Now I'll write the number ten on this other piece of paper. First I'll write a one because there's *one* group of ten, and then a zero because there are *no* ones left over."

Sitting at our desk in the back of the room, I kept an eye and ear on John's calendar proceedings. The first day of school was our first chance to see each other teach, to see and hear how we moved and talked with children. And it was quickly proving a valuable opportunity. I marveled at John's skilled touch with the activities and how he taught by example rather than by explanation. He had an expert way of integrating words, gestures, and visual props and keeping a steady, assured rapport with the entire class.

Just a few days earlier, John had set up the calendar and explained how the activities reinforced math, language arts, and science concepts along with a sense of classroom community. I now saw the calendar activities in action, and saw how John's attention to detail, his rapid pace, and his unexpected emphasis of certain words and concepts hooked the children in and propelled the activity forward.

And I sensed John's enjoyment, too, his "teaching pleasure" in the exactness and order of the various activities and his anticipation of the year-long, daily routine of the calendar. I also noticed how John made the most of the children's first exposure to the calendar activities, giving them just enough information and guidance to participate successfully and yet still have something to look forward to as an ongoing year-long activity. And John did it all with children he hardly knew.

John selected a different marker and crossed to the long chalkboard.

"Each day, we're going to write down how many days we've been in school," he said. "And by the end of the whole school year," John pointed to the long strip of adding machine paper stretching to the doorway, "we'll have a really long row of numbers. Since this is the first day of school, I'm going to write a one. And I'm writing it in what color?"

"Green," replied the class.

"Good. Tomorrow I'll write the next number in a different color and start a color pattern."

John capped the marker and backpedaled to the calendar.

"Boys and girls, look up here. This is the weather graph. Every day we're going to record the weather. I'll read these words: 'sunny, windy, cloudy, foggy, rainy.' Now we're going to take a vote. Look outside and then raise your hand if you think it's sunny outside."

The children craned their necks and squinted out the windows, all with great seriousness. John counted hands.

"Okay, put your hands down. How about windy? Cloudy? Foggy? Rainy?"

In typical first-grade fashion, not wanting to be left out and yet not quite understanding the concept of one-child-one-vote, many children voted two and even three times.

"Sunny wins!" John declared.

A few "sunny" children clenched their fists and looked at each other with satisfaction.

"Now I'm going to color the first 'sunny' box with what color marker?"

"Yellow," the class responded with an already confident it's-so-obvious tone.

"Let's look at the next graph. It's called a temperature graph. These words say: 'hot, warm, cold, cool.' Is it hot today? Warm?" Then John rubbed his hands along his forearms as if shivering. "Or cool like Mr. Sierra?" The children laughed at John's slapstick, but missed his play on words.

John put it to another vote. "Hot" won, and John colored the first "hot" square of the graph in red marker.

John paused and glanced at the hands of the big Art Deco–style clock above our heads. 9:50. Ten minutes until recess.

"Let's take them on a tour of the room," I suggested, and John agreed.

Like ducklings following their parents, the children trailed us as we showed them the Legos and building blocks and pattern blocks, the classroom library, listening center, "Helping Hands" job chart, "Student of the Week" area, board games, painting easels, writing center, group tables, and assorted materials on the bookshelves. The children listened patiently and obediently until Charles discovered Foo Foo, our class rabbit, behind our desk and the entire class surged toward the small cage.

"Can I feed it?"

"What's its name?"

"Ooh, I want to pet it."

"I want to pet it too!"

"Me too."

"Move! I can't see it."

"Can we let it out?"

Never mind the carefully displayed books in the library, the *Chutes and Ladders* and *Candyland* board games on the shelves, the smelly magic markers and typewriter in the writing center, all that John and I had arranged with specific educational purposes in mind—animate, potentially pettable, and lovable, our classroom rabbit stole the show on that first morning.

"Everybody take two giant steps back," John bellowed.

Keeping their eyes on Foo Foo, the class complied.

"This is Foo Foo, our class rabbit," John said. "You must be quiet, though, because you'll frighten him if you make too much noise. You'll get a chance to pet him once Foo Foo gets used to so many new people."

The 10:00 recess bell then rang, and we announced the magical phrase of "it's recess time." We instructed the children to stand "in a line" along the red tape we had placed on the floor stretching from the doorway to the windows. Charged with keeping "hands at sides" and "not talking," we led our class down the hallway, down the stairs to the first floor, out through the breezeway, and onto the playground. In ones, twos, and threes the children fanned out to play kickball, swing on the bars, run on the grass, climb the wooden play structures, and ride the tire swing.

It was their fifteen minutes of freedom after the first hour of school.

When the bell signaled the end of recess, the children followed our instructions and stood on the white line beside the handball wall. Although hot and sweaty, our class sandwiched themselves along less than half the line. Reassembling our duckling line, I took the lead and John the rear, and we began the long march upstairs.

Back in the classroom, I gathered the children on the rug for story.

Holding up the cover for all to see, I asked, "*Whose Mouse Are You?* Does anyone know this book?"

No one did.

I turned to the first page and propped the book open teacher-style with just my thumb and pinkie. The story was about a mouse facing the age-old quandary of a new baby sibling. The text was spare, with one or two lines per page.

"Whose mouse are you?" I read in my dramatic "story time" voice.

"Nobody's mouse," I answered on the second page.

"Where is your mother?" I asked on the third page.

The fourth page showed a double-spread illustration of a large cat with a mouse's tail trailing from its mouth.

"Inside the _____." I paused to let the children supply the missing word.

"Cat!" they said in unison.

"Where is your father?"

Turning the page, "Caught in a _____?"

"Trap!" the children said as they saw the father trapped in a cage.

"Where is your sister? Far from home. Where is your brother? I have none. What will you do? Shake my mother out of the _____."

"Cat!" cried the children when they saw the mouse shake the big fat cat, whose eyes tripled in number with the ferocity of the mouse's efforts.

"Free my father from the _____."

"Trap!" shouted the class; the mouse was sawing through the trap.

"Find my sister and bring her _____."

"Home." The mouse had arrived via a hot air balloon to rescue his sister.

"Wish for a brother as I have none. Now whose mouse are you? My mother's mouse, she loves me _____."

"So."

"My father's mouse from head to _____."

Sensing the rhyme, the class answered, "Toe."

"My sister's mouse, she loves me too. My brother's mouse . . . Your brother's mouse? My brother's mouse—he's brand _____."

"New!" The last page showed the mouse with his new baby brother.

No sooner had I closed the book then Warren waved his arm.

"Last year in kindergarten," Warren said as he took the liberty of calling on himself, "my teacher let kids get up in front of the class and say their favorite part of the story."

"That's a good idea, Warren, but I don't want people to get up."

Warren crinkled his nose in disagreement, but smiled as I called on him first. He stood to face the class.

"My favorite part is when the mouse comes in the balloon. He looks like he's really flying. I wish I could do that. It looks like fun. And—"

Not wanting to lose the children's interest, I asked, "Do you know what kind of balloon it is?"

Warren shook his head and pursed his lips, disappointed that he didn't know the answer in front of his new peers.

"Does anyone know? . . . No? It's a hot air balloon."

I pointed out the sandbags in the illustration and explained how they acted as a ballast.

When Michele and Eugene shared their favorite parts, I noticed they focused more on the illustrations than the text. I asked the next few children to say whether their favorite part was "before" or "after" the picture open at the moment. The children knew the sequence of the pictures better than I, and more than once delighted in correcting me, "No, no, not that way! The other way!"

Putting the book down, I nodded to John and we passed the baton again.

"Boys and girls," John said again with a quick clap of his hands. "Since this is your classroom, Mr. Meier and I want you to make your own rules so that we can all get along together this year. Who has a rule that would help us get along?"

Rule-setting is a common practice in classrooms in order to promote prosocial behavior, but John and I wanted the children to play an integral role in the process. The children took their cue and eagerly participated in the rule-making as John wrote their suggestions on a large piece of chart paper clipped to the blackboard.

With a softness he would retain all year, Matthew said, "You shouldn't hit anybody because they could get hurt."

"Yeah," Charles added with his already unique sense of humor, "and no kicking them or punching them or giving any karate chops."

"And I don't think," Michele said with maturity, "kids should tease other kids because they'll get their feelings hurt."

John synthesized all the suggestions, retaining the children's original intent and language.

> Don't hit nobody.
> No spitting.
> Don't bother people when they're doing their work.
> Share all the things you work with.
> Don't hit.
> Don't tease.
> Be nice.
> No stealing.
> Don't kick.
> No kung fu or karate.
> Don't make people feel bad.
> Ask someone to play if they don't have somebody to play with.
> Don't get into no trouble. (my favorite)

John stepped back from the list and studied it as if it were a painting.

"These are good rules. But there're too many of them. Also, some of the rules talk about the same thing. So we need to *group* them together and make just a few rules. Watch what I'm going to do. Is everybody watching?"

John paused to make sure.

"This rule about 'no kicking' is like this rule about 'no karate.' Why? Because they both have to do with hurting people physically. So I'm going to circle both rules with a blue marker. Okay, now, see this rule about 'being nice' and this other rule about 'not teasing'? These two are alike because they both involve people's feelings. I'll circle both rules with a red marker."

John circled and grouped the remaining rules.

"Now let's go back and look at all the blue rules. What's one rule we could write that would say something about all the blue rules?"

No one raised a hand.

"This is hard. Since all the blue rules have to do with getting hurt on the outside of our bodies, let's write, 'Don't hurt anybody.'"

John continued the process until he crystallized a final list.

1. Play fair.
2. Do not damage anything.
3. Take turns talking.
4. Keep your hands and feet to yourself.
5. Don't hurt other people's feelings.

John taped the final list to the wall, where it would remain for the rest of the year.

It was then almost 11:30 and time for recess and lunch. John told the children to get their lunches and fall in line again along the red tape.

On his way out, Warren held his lunch aloft.

"I have sweets, John and Daniel. But don't worry. I won't get hyper."

John and I laughed.

After walking the children outside, John and I barely had time to tidy the classroom, review the afternoon schedule, and eat our lunch before the 12:05 bell sent us back down the hallway, munching our half-eaten sandwiches as we walked.

Back in the classroom, John turned off the lights and told the children to put their heads down on the tables "for five minutes of rest." The children leaned and squirmed on their forearms; they were too excited to rest.

John turned on the lights and announced, "I'm going to pick the quietest group to get a book from our classroom library and read quietly at your seat. This is our U.S.S.R. [for "Uninterrupted Sustained Silent Reading"], or silent reading time. You can trade your book with someone at your table or get a new one from the library, but you can only have *one* book at a time. You can also share a book, but only two people to a book."

Our first version of U.S.S.R. was sustained but not silent as children talked about their books and "read" the pictures out loud.

The afternoon went as smoothly as the morning. At the end of the day, when we announced "free choice time," another magical phrase for children, the children scurried to their already-favorite activities around the classroom.

Steven and Joshua, who seemed to know each other from kindergarten, built towers out of the brightly colored wooden pattern blocks. David built a network of roads on the rug with the wooden blocks. Deborah, Gina, and Janet took to the easels, dripping and splattering greens and yellows and blues onto both the newsprint and the floor. Joey and Charles and a few other boys returned to their early-morning Lego work, constructing spaceships and helicopter gunships that they zoomed at low altitude above the rug. Given a measure of freedom for choosing activities and peer partners, there were no squabbles, only ample noise and movement.

Fifteen minutes before our daily 2:20 dismissal, I gathered the class on the rug for a rereading of *Whose Mouse Are You?* The children easily supplied the now-familiar missing words. Just before the bell, John and I reassembled the children along the red line, resumed our doorway posts, and handed out the principal's first-day newsletter, which the children promptly rolled into makeshift trumpets and baseball bats. With two dozen "good-byes" and "see you tomorrows," we ended the first day of our shared classroom.

Like a couple discussing the departed party guests, John and I reviewed our first day. We were pleased. John and I had achieved most of our first-day goals—we met our students and many of their families, learned names, oriented the children to the classroom and school, introduced important classroom routines like morning meeting and getting into line, and engaged the children in activities and our budding classroom community.

The unexpected and unplanned-for also added to the day's success. Charles's early-morning humor eased our nervousness, Amanda's strong reading of the morning message provided a peer model of reading success and power for the other children, Warren's suggestion to share "favorite parts" enriched our first story time, and the discovery of Foo Foo garnered everybody's attention.

The planned and the unplanned, the expected and the unexpected, all provided us with the early feeling of getting our classroom and year off to a good start. John and I were also simply relieved to start teaching together, pleased by the opportunity to teach and interact with our students.

It is rare in schools for teachers to observe colleagues teaching, and even more rare for teachers to co-teach. Early on our first day together, as I sat in the back of the room, I observed how the nuances of John's teaching contributed to his success—how he maintained eye contact with the class during the calendar activities, kept up a lively pace to keep the children focused and interested, modulated the pitch of his voice for emphasis, and demonstrated important aspects of the activities with examples rather than explanations.

It is also unusual for teachers to comment directly on each other's teaching. It felt good when John said he liked the way I read *Whose Mouse Are You?*

and engaged the children in telling their favorite parts of the story. He also liked the tone of voice I used in addressing the children.

In turn, I told John how much I liked how he made the rule-making session one part community-building (involving the children in the process of making the rules), one part math lesson (regrouping the categories of rules), and one part language arts lesson (translating talk into writing and reading). I also liked how he joked with the class when he rubbed his forearms and said "Cool, like Mr. Sierra" during the calendar activities; the humor helped ease everybody's nervousness.

The first day of school brings challenges for teachers, children, and their families. Like any first-time experience, and especially given the special place of first grade in children's school lives, the day has its own fears and hopes and expectations. The children faced a transition from summer to school, from the world outside to the world of the classroom, from familiar and comfortable social relations to the newer and more fragile bonds as teachers and students.

John and I also found the first day of school a challenge. In my previous teaching position at a private school in Boston, on the first day of school I met all the children's parents and they lingered in my classroom to ease their children's transition into first grade. At Mayfield, a diverse group of adults came to our doorway—fathers, mothers, grandmothers, big sisters, and neighbors—and they didn't linger in the room. In addition, some students were dropped off outside the building by their parents, or arrived by school bus and found their own way up to our classroom. Some of our perceptions of our students' families, which would influence our teaching over the course of the year, were rooted in the early moments of the first day of school.

Given the diversity of students and their families—all with their own respective histories and experiences with schools and schooling—we all met and came together as strangers. It is one of the ironies of modern schooling that perfect strangers, often from diverse social and cultural histories, are asked to become "quick intimates" within the close confines of the classroom. It's no easy task, and one rarely addressed in depth for teachers and families.

And teaching at a new school, new to the intricacies of job sharing, John and I also didn't know each other well. On the first day of school, we had a better idea of how to interact and work with the students than we did with each other. The first day of school, then, was our first experience as two adult learners learning from each other. In the process, we couldn't wait and take our time; John and I had to implement what we planned, think on our feet and adjust to the unexpected, and set in motion the kind of classroom world we envisioned.

And in doing so, we asked a lot of the children. When we peeled away the layers of the day's first minutes, the children had confronted a whirl of people and directions and activities. Arriving at our classroom door, they said good-bye to their families, met their teachers, found their name tags, selected a cubby, chose an activity, interacted with peers, cleaned up, and sat in a circle on the rug for something called "morning meeting." Much of this was familiar school routine for many of our students, but they had to begin all over again as it all took on a different flavor and pace and color in our classroom.

The "hidden curriculum," the unstated and yet important rules and expectations in classrooms, is often talked about as a static and stable element of classrooms across grade levels and situations. But it isn't. It moves and changes. New to Room 201, to John and me, to the demands of first grade, our students confronted brand-new expectations and messages. When I read the morning message, I did it my way; I asked the class to read the message on the board, the hidden curriculum of the moment shifting to mean that I indirectly wanted them to remain seated, follow my left index finger as I pointed, start with the first word on the top left and stop with the last at bottom right, keep pace (but not overshadow) my voice, and have a beginning awareness that what we were reading had a meaning and a message. And I expected the children to do all this without my directly saying so; they had to watch my lead, and follow my examples and actions.

After the children left for the day, I bent down to pick up the stray crayons and paper scraps from the floor. John let Foo Foo out for a well-deserved run around the classroom. We could hear the distant shouts of children let free from the first day of school. Pleased with our first day of school, we were eager for the second.

Settling In–Curriculum and Classroom Organization

Once upon a time there was a home.

by Matthew

The classroom should have the personal imprint of the teacher. Do not impose it on the children, but make it clear what you value.

Bruno Bettelheim

I first met John at the punch bowl. A year before we started teaching together, we attended an orientation for new graduate students in education at a university in the San Francisco Bay area. I liked John immediately. As we sipped the too-sweet punch, we talked about our professional experiences and interests. John had taught first grade for three years as a Spanish/English bilingual teacher in Phoenix, and I had taught first grade for three years at a private school in Boston. We also discovered that we were both interested in children's literature and loved the special challenge of helping children learn to read and write.

I didn't see John in the fall, though, because he took the semester off to work and support his family. In late January, when we enrolled in the same course, we saw each other again. During class breaks, we walked to the vending machines and continued our initial conversation about teaching and education. One day we discussed our job plans for the upcoming year, when John suddenly became excited.

"What do you think of this?," he said with a clap of his hands, "Why don't we work together? We both want to teach but can't do it full-time. Why not job share? I know people who did it in Arizona and they liked it. All we have to do is advertise ourselves as two male teachers who want to teach first grade, and they'll snap us up in a minute."

I liked John's idea. I, too, had seen job sharing work; two of my private school colleagues had successfully job shared a first-grade position. I also found graduate school isolating, and missed teaching children and the hustle-bustle of school life.

But a recent co-teaching experience had been unpleasant and short-lived. After my third year of private school teaching, I wanted a new professional challenge, to teach in a public school. I accepted a full-time position co-teaching two classes of sixth graders in a Boston public school. It was a challenge. Through a long fall, I fretted over student discipline problems, lack of communication and camaraderie with my co-teacher, and the general feeling of isolation in a new, large school. The experience not only taught me that co-teaching is hard work, but that the quality of cooperation and communication between the two teachers is essential. So when John mentioned sharing the same classroom, I felt nervous and gun-shy about the even more involved job sharing.

17

I was also a little uneasy about working with John. Clearly we shared a love of first graders and teaching six-year-olds to read and write. Yet I wasn't sure John and I were compatible enough; although we didn't know each other well, I sensed that our personalities and personal backgrounds were too different.

In our graduate school class on the education of linguistic minorities, our differences surfaced. In class discussions, sometimes heated and tense as white and Chicano students argued over issues of ethnicity, power, class, and school achievement, I was quiet and John outspoken. He talked candidly and poignantly about growing up Chicano in the Southwest. He described one childhood incident in which he and a friend tried to rub off their dark brown skin with bleach and a rag in order to be white. I admired John's determination in facing challenges I had never encountered, and the open way he discussed and confronted controversial issues.

Yet I stalled on job sharing with John; I still felt that we were too different and that it would make for a difficult job share.

By late spring, when I still hadn't found a teaching partner, our department secretary walked into my office.

"Dan," she said. "I heard you were looking for a teaching partner. I want you to meet an Arizona Language Arts Teacher of the Year: John Sierra."

John rounded the doorway and gave a sheepish smile as if to say, "I tried to tell her." There was just something in John's smile that pushed my doubts aside, and I decided to give the job share a try. John and I shook hands and sat down to map out a strategy for finding a shared job.

Three weeks later, in our first contact with a school, we interviewed for a first-grade position at Mayfield School, a kindergarten through grade three public school in an urban district. In our application, we made it clear that we wanted to share the job and each teach half-time.

John and I met at the principal's office for our interview. The secretary introduced herself as Cindy and said the principal would be with us shortly. John and I inspected each other's interview costumes; without prior consultation, we both wore self-ironed khaki trousers and ties. John looked particularly uncomfortable with his tie and fidgeted with the knot. I shifted my feet. There was no place to sit, and standing off to the side, we felt more like two children in trouble than prospective teachers.

A woman opened a back door.

"Hi, I'm Marian. I'm the principal."

With smiles all round, we shook hands over the counter.

"Your interview will be held in the library."

As she led us down the hallway, Marian said, "You know, the interview committee is mainly interested in knowing how you two plan to share the position and work together as a team."

Thankful for the last-second tip, John and I dropped back a step or two, and rehearsed in whispers the main points of our sketchy job share plan.

The committee—Marian, three teachers, and a parent—peppered us with questions, many of which concerned co-teaching:

"How will you share the teaching responsibilities? Who's going to teach what and when?"

"As two teachers job sharing, how will you communicate with each other and how will you keep parents informed?"

"Reading is so important in first grade. How will you teach it? What materials and methods will you use?"

"We have a diverse student composition at this school. How will you manage a classroom with a wide range of abilities? And since there are two of you, how will you coordinate discipline?"

"I have a child with learning difficulties who will be in your class. What kinds of things will you do to help him?"

In our early answers, John and I talked about our past teaching experiences. We didn't plan it this way; it was simply a natural way to portray ourselves as strong and capable teachers. Then, answer by answer, we slowly talked more as a "we" and as a unified partnership. It was harder, but the formal interview helped by challenging us to articulate our educational philosophies and beliefs into a shared vision for our classroom-to-be.

The interview also marked the formal beginning of what would become an intimate professional and personal relationship. It was the first test of our budding partnership, and like two-man tag-team wrestlers, when one of us fumbled an answer or sounded unsure, we came to each other's rescue. The interview also forced us to listen to each other, to sense the pauses and the hesitations in each other's speech and mannerisms, and gauge when and how we could help each other. Although we didn't realize it at the time, John and I were learning about each other as individuals as we learned about each other as teachers. In a little model of adult learning, we were two teachers learning about each other in the process of describing a shared classroom.

"We'll integrate traditional subjects like science and social studies into theme units," I explained in response to a question on our curriculum. "For example, our first theme of 'All About Me' will focus on the children themselves. We'll explore what they like to do and what interests them. It's a good way for children to feel special and to learn about each other . . . "

I paused, unsure how to flesh out the next unit, and on cue John picked up the tag.

". . . and then we'll move on to studying the children's families, neighborhoods, and communities. It's important to start with the children like Dan said—who they are and what they like to do—and then branch out. As we do so, we'll also bring in math and reading and writing activities. We'll integrate it. For example, we will make a graph of the children's favorite things to do at home and count and compare totals."

There were moments, though, when I found myself tempering John's statements; I sensed that to be hired, we needed to present a balanced approach between a traditional emphasis on teaching skills and the more current emphasis on child-centered and hands-on teaching. I also knew from experience that teachers have a tremendous amount of freedom to teach as they wish once they close the classroom door.

On the ever-controversial topic of teaching spelling, John declared, "I've never seen a formal spelling program work and I don't see the point of teacher-prepared weekly spelling tests. They're just words in isolation. I believe children learn to spell within the context of their own writing. I believe in promoting children's invented spelling and helping them from where they are developmentally."

Without appearing to disagree, I made a plug for some direct spelling instruction.

"Yes, we are concerned with children learning to spell correctly," I added. "It's just that we don't want to do it in isolation. It's important for children to learn the words they want and need in their writing. Dictation is also a good activity for young children to learn to spell correctly."

On beginning reading instruction, another perennially controversial subject, John stated, "I've never seen the point of teaching phonics. Children need to learn how to read whole texts and books. They don't need language broken up into little tiny pieces. They need real language from the world. I've found that children learn to read when they get interested in a story or a book and want to learn how to read it."

I slipped in a good word for phonics.

"Phonics teaching has a role. Not, like John said, when it's used to break up language into meaningless pieces, but as a way to show children how language is constructed. It's another useful tool in an eclectic approach to teaching reading. Not all children learn the same way, and so we'll use a variety of methods and materials."

There were other moments when I felt that John and I were far apart in terms of educational beliefs and philosophies.

"I strongly believe in home visits," John said in response to a question on promoting parent–teacher communication. "In Arizona, I found that early contact with children and families in their homes before the start of the school year was a great help. Growing up in the Southwest, and speaking Spanish, when I went into homes and visited families, they could relate to me and I could relate to them. This kind of out-of-school contact helped them feel more comfortable with me and with school."

Although I understood John's intentions, I had no interest in visiting children's homes; I thought it could potentially embarrass both the families and me, and hoped the interview committee wouldn't ask my opinion. They didn't.

John and I improvised our way through the rest of the interview, and two weeks later, we were hired.

John was right; two male teachers who wanted to work with young children were seen as an advantage, a plus outweighing the unknowns and potential drawbacks of job sharing. As newly hired ".50 FTE" or fifty-percent employees, we qualified for full medical and partial dental benefits from the district. John and I signed our contracts, thankful for the steady income and the new teaching opportunity.

On a hot afternoon in late August, John and I loaded my car with boxes and drove to Mayfield. We were moving into our classroom. Tucked into a sunny residential neighborhood between two busy thoroughfares, Mayfield comprised an entire square block. Bordered by single-family wood and stucco houses, and located within walking distance of the city's downtown, Mayfield had occupied the same site for nearly 100 years.

Originally built in the late 1800s as a two-room school, Mayfield expanded to accommodate the city's rapidly growing population of school-age children. Mayfield continued to grow over the years, and the existing school building was constructed in 1952. When John and I were hired, the school site comprised 17 classrooms, a large auditorium, cafeteria, and a playground area with grass, asphalt, basketball hoops, and climbing structures. After school, the playground doubled as a community park, and one basketball court filled with a regular game of adults playing in the afternoons and early evenings. Mobile classrooms at the edge of the playground housed preschool classes administered by the district's early childhood program.

A long open-air courtyard in the middle of the school, hidden from the street and tucked between the two wings of the school, contained the school's farm and garden. Staffed by a specialist teacher, the farm and garden program enabled each class to tend a small garden plot of vegetables and flowers and care for a large collection of ducks, chickens, hens, rabbits, and goats. The program, supported by the school's PTA and special district funds, continued Mayfield's long-standing tradition of school and community gardening.

John and I parked at the end of the block. Through the dry, crinkly leaves of the maple trees lining the street, we gazed up at our second-floor classroom. In its earliest days, Mayfield was a "neighborhood school," drawing its small number of students from the white, lower- to middle-class families in the immediate neighborhood. As the city's population increased, especially during and after World War II when new families moved to the San Francisco Bay area to work in the wartime industries, Mayfield's student composition also became more diverse. During the district's school desegregation efforts in the 1960s, Mayfield remained one of the city's most racially diverse schools. Over the next 20 years, while some white students and their families left for the suburbs or enrolled in private schools, Mayfield continued to maintain its ethnic mix.

When John and I were hired, the city's public kindergarten through grade 12 schools were approximately 41% African American, 39% white, 10% Latino, 9% Asian, and 1% Native American. The ethnic composition of Mayfield, serving 350 kindergarten through grade 3 students, was 54% African American, 36% white, 4% Latino, 4% Asian, and 2% Native American and other ethnicities. Approximately 45% of the children qualified for the school's federally funded free breakfast and lunch program, and a number of these children attended the state and federally funded before- and afterschool day care programs on-site.

In our particular first-grade class, John and I averaged 27 students over the course of the year. In an unusual but not uncommon gender imbalance, we had 19 boys and 8 girls. Eighteen of the students were African American, five white, two of mixed white/African American ancestry, one Latina, and one South American. About half of our class qualified for the free breakfast and lunch program, and several attended the day care program. Roughly a third of our students lived within walking distance of Mayfield. The rest of the children lived farther away, but still in Mayfield's prescribed attendance zone, and were driven to school by parents or took the school bus. A few students, registered with a special interdistrict transfer, were "out of district" and lived in neighboring cities.

Mayfield's staff and faculty were also a diverse group. John and I noticed the mix at our first all-staff meeting attended by the 12 classroom teachers, principal, secretary, custodians, instructional assistants, and specialist teachers. Headed by a veteran African American principal, Mayfield's staff represented a range of ages, ethnic backgrounds, and years of teaching experience. Unusual for primary schools, the faculty also included two other male teachers beside John and myself. We were the only job sharing or co-teaching team on the faculty. And working with Belva, our instructional assistant, who was African American and a veteran teacher at Mayfield and in the district, our particular team was the most mixed at the school.

Racially, economically, and socially, our classroom and school were a microcosm of the rapidly changing demographic picture of California's schools. In terms of the children, their families, and the staff, Mayfield was the most culturally varied school John and I had worked at. John, coming from a bilingual experience in the Southwest, had never worked with African American or white children. I had worked with predominantly middle- to upper-middle-class white children at a private school in Boston, and had limited experience with an ethnically diverse group of children and adults. And given our respective life histories and previous teaching experiences, for the first time John and I would be in the "minority" in terms of cultural background within our own classroom. Before we started the year at Mayfield, John and I had little idea of the challenges ahead in forging a viable classroom community from a diversity of children and adults.

I popped open the trunk of my car. John and I sighed at the sweaty prospect of carrying the boxes upstairs. With a "one, two, three," we hoisted the two biggest boxes on our shoulders, crossed the playground, and started a slow ascent to our second-floor classroom. In the hallway we slowed to greet our new colleagues, and taking a peek into their classrooms, we were relieved that we weren't the only ones not ready for the first day of school.

At the end of the long hallway, John and I let the boxes slip to the floor. I reached for my new district-issue Schlage key and unlocked the door to Room 201. We were moving in. John propped the door onto its catch, and I walked across the greenish-blue linoleum floor to the long bank of windows on the far wall. I gave each metal handle a quarter-turn to the right to let in the warm breeze. We opened the small rectangular windows in the hallway for a cross-breeze. The open windows brought in sounds of the farm and garden below, the rooster crowing and the chickens squawking. We liked the country feel in an urban setting.

After another trip to the car, John and I dropped the boxes and shared a laugh about the rumor that our classroom was jinxed. We'd heard that no teacher in recent memory had lasted more than a year in the room. As often happens to new teachers, we were assigned the room, but we liked it. Sunny and warm, the room was spacious and rectangular-shaped, with well-built and thoughtfully designed furnishings more often found in older school buildings. Nothing plastic. Nothing flimsy.

Surveying the room from the one doorway, two long green chalkboards with ribbed wooden ledges spanned the two walls to the right. Permanent shelves, adjustable and at child level, lined most of the long wall beneath the windows. Two large wooden closets, several cabinets and bookshelves, a metal sink and drinking faucet, and a counter area comprised the left wall. Five bulletin boards, four inside and one in the hallway, provided ample display space for children's work. A little direct sunlight entered from the hallway, and the tall windows provided ample indirect light.

The only other prize besides the room itself was a large kidney-shaped table, which John considered a real coup.

"I've wanted one of these tables for a long time. They're great for work-ing with reading groups. No one's taking this," John said as he placed a heavy box on it for safekeeping.

There were only a few materials left for us. First-year and new teachers are often hired late in the summer, and upon arrival their assigned classrooms can look like apartments hastily left by the previous tenant. There is also the unspoken expectation that new teachers should take the initiative in securing their desired furniture and supplies beyond what's left in the room. As John and I knew from experience, good relations with the school custodian and secretary go a long way in setting up a classroom.

Our remaining furniture consisted of several individual student desks, a two-tiered cabinet with 20 cubbyholes, a few odd-sized tables, an ancient shag rug, 2 standing dividers, 4 beanbag chairs, a teacher's desk, and a dozen or so unmatched chairs. The cupboards were bare save for a messy mix of paper, scissors, pencils, pens, and a pile of third-grade reading and math textbooks.

On our second day of moving in, John brought a portable radio and the beat of a local jazz station echoed across the bare linoleum. Like newly-weds moving into their first home, John and I parceled out the storage space drawer by drawer, cabinet by cabinet, closet by closet. As we unpacked our boxes, we spread out a buffet of tools of the teaching trade—children's literature books, professional books, math manipulatives, games, folders of dittos and worksheets, magazines, homemade activity kits, flash cards, samples of student work, charts, graphs, posters, a wooden puppet theatre.

I expressed mock surprise at the sheer volume.

"Maybe I should get rid of some of this stuff," I said.

"It's not worth it," John said, tossing an empty box on top of the cabi-nets. "It's all part of teaching—you hold onto your stuff forever, just in case you might use it once."

As John and I sorted and stored our materials, we held an impromptu show-and-tell session. John held up a book written and illustrated by a former student.

"Dan, you're going to love this one. It's Julio's story. He let me keep it because I liked it so much. It's just incredible. You're not going to believe this story."

John read the story in its original Spanish and translated it into English after each page. The story was about a boy and his father fishing, and how father and son finally work together to catch a fish. John read it and pointed to the pictures just as if there were a room full of young children listening. He shook his head when he finished.

"Isn't this amazing? Just incredible. He describes the relationship between the son and his father so beautifully. He was so proud of this story."

The way John read the story, with feeling and warmth, I felt that Julio had just finished the story and brought it to John.

"Here's a magazine I made with my class," I said. "The kids wrote all the stories and then I cut and pasted them into a published book."

I then shared a few selections. I was proud of the varied genres in which my first graders wrote: stories, movie reviews, fables, cartoons, and advertisements.

I was glad that our sharing was informal and not competitive. I sensed John's admiration for his student's story and his love of his students' writing. In revisiting my students' writing, I remembered how much I enjoyed teaching young children to write.

Underlying the warmth of our professional connections, though, I was still aware of our differences. In our previous experiences, John had taught working-class children in Phoenix and I wealthier children in Boston. John couldn't believe my small classes of 15 children; John's averaged over 30 students and their parents were miners and farmers who spoke little English. After sharing our former students' work, I sensed that our previous teaching experiences aligned with our personal backgrounds—our upbringing connected with the kinds of students and families we had worked with. I started to doubt again whether our shared teaching plan would work. But I reminded myself that with effort and care we could both learn and grow in this new teaching opportunity.

Elementary school classrooms are the most crowded places children inhabit. Nowhere else—bus, train, home—do so many children crowd into the same small space for long periods of time. Given this parameter of modern schooling, John and I knew that the physical arrangement of a classroom is a powerful influence on the quality of life for students and teachers.

As John and I talked about the kind of classroom we wanted, we agreed on the value of young children talking, sharing, and interacting as they worked. We believed that daily, sustained opportunities for social interaction fostered positive peer relations and contributed to children's academic development as part of an evolving intellectual community. John and I disagreed, though, on the optimal room arrangement to support this kind of social networking.

"I used tables in Arizona," John said. "They help kids work together and share, and build a sense of community by getting groups of children to cooperate."

"You can make small groups by clustering three or four individual desks together," I countered. "That's what I used to do. It's a good way for children to have their own personal space and yet at the same time work with peers."

The tables versus desks debate never reached a higher level of educational debate; in conducting our two-man reconnaissance raids around Mayfield, scavenging closets and storage areas, we uncovered several large tables but only a few individual desks.

"I know you want desks, Dan," John said, "but we're not going to do any better than this. We're new teachers; we get stuck with the stuff nobody else wants."

John predicted we might get 30 students.

"But you never know," he said with a knowing public school wink. "We might get more at any time of the year."

Figuring six children per table, we selected the five best tables, scraped the stubborn glue spots with razor blades, scoured the crayon and marker stains with Bon Ami powder, and tightened the loose legs with John's Allen wrench. We pushed and pulled the tables into various configurations as we searched for the arrangement that would provide maximum maneuvering room, accessibility, and social contact. We finally decided on a temporary arrangement, postponing something more permanent until we arranged the rest of the classroom.

Once we agreed on the tables, other decisions came easily. To promote cooperative learning and small-group cohesion, we made five signs designating the "blue diamond," "red circle," "yellow square," "green triangle," and "purple rectangle" table groups. John believed that group names would give the children a sense of small-group identity and help with the all-important transitions for a large group of eager and fast-moving six-year-olds. I liked the idea.

At the local variety store, we bought five plastic tubs and filled them with pencils, small glue bottles, scissors, crayons, and markers that Cindy had placed in our "201" cardboard box in the office. Although Mayfield had a supply closet for teachers from which we could request materials, we started out the year with a box of supplies.

John and I decided that the children's work materials, such as writing journals and reading books, would go in their individual cubbies; when we wanted to collect their work, we could easily retrieve it from the cubbies. We also agreed to store other materials, such as literature logs and reading books, behind the kidney-shaped table, which would serve as our instructional "command center."

Early Thursday morning, five days before the first day of school, John lay on his back straightening the table legs when Joyce, a first-grade colleague, appeared at the doorway. Her black hair tied up in a bun, Joyce stroked a large black and white rabbit softly cradled in her left arm.

"You guys need a furry friend? This is Foo Foo," she said.

Like a mechanic coming out from under a car, John slid along the floor.

"You sure you don't want it?" he asked.

"I'm sure. A former student gave it to me at the end of last year, and the number of animals in my room has reached capacity," Joyce said.

"What do you think?" John asked me.

"Let's take it," I said. "We could do with some more animal life in here."

We put Foo Foo (a name John disliked) in a small metal cage behind our desk. John bought a plastic tub and kitty litter, and was determined to house-train Foo Foo so he could wander the classroom.

By the fourth full day of moving, John and I were pleased with our progress. Our arrangement of the furniture and physical space provided concrete evidence of our shared classroom taking shape.

We weren't even disheartened when a colleague stopped by, looked at our walls and table arrangement, and said with a smile, "Oh, a male teachers' room."

"And just what do you mean by that?" I said.

"Yeah," John said in a show of male teacher bonding, "what do you mean?"

She laughed, "Oh, all right, I take it back. It looks great."

With the first day of school fast approaching, and having spent most of our time moving in and arranging our classroom, John and I still needed to discuss and decide on important aspects of our curriculum and classroom organization.

First, we debated the relative merits of various teaching schedules. I told John about two of my former colleagues who had job shared and chose a daily morning/afternoon split, with one teacher responsible for teaching language arts and social studies in the morning, and the other teacher doing math and science in the afternoon. At their lunchtime switch, the teachers met in the classroom to exchange news. The teachers also kept track of important classroom events and information in a shared journal, which remained in the classroom. Both teachers shared parent conferences, report writing, and recess duty and faculty meetings. After some initial skepticism, the school's administration and parents viewed the job share as a success.

I knew of other job sharing possibilities. Two kindergarten teachers taught consecutive whole days. They particularly liked this arrangement because it afforded large chunks of time both away from and in school. Another job sharing team alternated teaching the entire school week. They co-taught and planned curriculum on the afternoon of their once-a-week switch, and believed this schedule provided time to work on long-term classroom projects and plan together at school.

I found little literature on job sharing except for one book with a section on teachers. The two teachers profiled chose a morning/afternoon split, one teaching language arts, reading, and spelling in the morning and the other teaching math, physical education, science, and history in the afternoon. Both teachers liked the job share; it afforded personal time away from school and offered their students the creativity and energy of two fresh and enthusiastic teachers. It also enabled a young, new teacher to learn from a veteran partner, who in turn was rejuvenated by the younger teacher's energy and interest.

John and I decided to teach consecutive whole days. It would give us time to concentrate on our graduate work and also enable us to work on classroom projects over the course of two or three days. John would teach Mondays and Tuesdays, I'd teach Wednesdays and Thursdays, and we would alternate all day Friday every other week.

We also kept our initial plan to co-teach the breadth of the first grade curriculum, both of us teaching language arts and math and integrating science and social studies into themes such as "All About Me." We would keep in touch by writing in a shared teaching journal, and John bought a handsome journal covered with Italian-marbled paper for our desk. John and I also agreed to talk on the phone and meet outside school to plan and coordinate lessons.

Moving in, meeting colleagues, arranging our classroom, and making decisions about our co-teaching schedule—John and I accomplished a great deal before the first day of school. But a range of decisions remained unaddressed: certain curriculum specifics (did we want to use a children's literature book to start the school year?); a discipline system (John favored a "stop light" chart that I didn't like), and a homework policy (we did agree on parents reading a library book to their children in preparation for a Friday reading conference at school). All too aware of these shortcomings, and short on time, John and I comforted each other with a philosophical "let's decide as we get to know the children" and a pragmatic "we'll figure it out as we go."

On the Thursday evening before the first day of school, Marian arranged a potluck dinner for families and children to meet the mostly new first-grade teachers. Another colleague, Emily, was also new to Mayfield and the district. When I arrived at the school's cafeteria for the potluck, I quickly found John and we nervously piled spaghetti on our plates before meeting our families.

We happened to start with Joshua and his parents, Virginia and George, who held a baby clad in a tie-dyed jumpsuit. They were a good first family to meet; friendly and talkative, they immediately put us at ease and made us feel comfortable. After a few minutes, I struck out on my own and as I looked back, I saw John laugh and place a friendly hand on George's shoulder.

I then met Matthew, with thick black hair and a shy smile, as he sat with his mother at one of the long white cafeteria tables. Quiet at first, Matthew became more animated with his mother's encouragement, and as John joined us, we continued to talk over ice cream and coffee.

Joe and Karen were our next parents. With long hair in a ponytail and tattoos up and down his forearms, Joe looked young. He told us he was a pipe fitter on ships and he'd just been offered a well-paying job in the Middle East. Just then a tall boy with a streak of black hair rushed by.

Joe held out his arm like a train crossing gate.

"Whoa there, Charles. I want you to meet your teachers, Daniel and John."

Charles looked at me. Then at John.

"What? *Two* teachers? Where am I? *The Twilight Zone?*" He tossed his hands into the air and ran back outside.

"He's a good kid," Joe said. "He just watches too much television and sometimes has a hard time concentrating in school. His kindergarten teacher, though, was strict with him and it paid off."

John and I met our four or five remaining students and their families, talking and sipping more coffee until Marian flicked the lights off and on and thanked everybody for coming. John and I helped our new colleagues clear the food and wipe and fold up the tables, and we carried our talk about children and school out into the parking lot and the cool of the September evening.

At eight o'clock on the eve of the first day of school, John and I put the finishing touches on our classroom. Before leaving, we gave the room a final look-over. The group table signs, suspended from the ceiling with fishing tackle, twirled slowly. The larger-than-child-size stuffed brown bear, which I bought for $5 at the Salvation Army, sat upright in our classroom library. Dozens of books lined the bookshelves and chalkboard ledges. John's tall fish tank, the small orange fish swimming in circles, bubbled away in the corner of the library. Five new boxes of smelly magic markers sat on five pieces of drawing paper on the kidney-shaped table. Foo Foo was tucked in for the night in his cage. Fresh pieces of newsprint covered the two painting easels at the art center. Two pink 6′ x 9′ rugs (I brought one and John the other) were taped together to form our group meeting area. Brand-new Crayola crayons and fat blue pencils, "DIXON•Laddie•3304 School/Supply" engraved in gold on the side, sat in the five plastic tubs. Thirty small chairs awaited the imminent arrival of as many excited, fidgeting six-year-old bodies.

We were ready for the first day of school. I pulled out the key, let the door swing shut, and John and I headed down the hallway for a well-deserved bite to eat.

3

Astronauts and Hammerhead Spaceships– Getting to Know Students

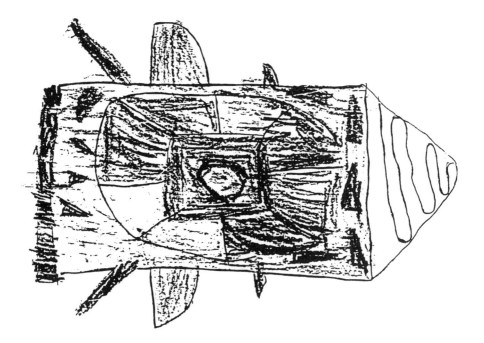

This is the Hammerhead spaceship.

by Joshua

It seems to me that the tasks which one sets for oneself and the children to accomplish, in poetry, drama, filmmaking, painting, or whatever, grow directly out of the unique local situation in which the teacher finds himself and out of the unique personalities of the children. . . . There is no such thing as a "creativity curriculum" divorced from personalities and social context.

Phillip Lopate, *Being with Children*

Teachers face the difficult professional and personal task of getting to know a large group of students quickly. It's an important challenge, for the ultimate success of a classroom community hinges on the quality and the strength of the social and personal bonds formed between children and teachers. It is on this foundation that students trust teachers, and upon which teachers personalize and engage individual students in the classroom curriculum and community.

At the beginning of our school year, though, John and I didn't know the students and they didn't know us. We not only had to earn each other's trust, but the journey involved a muddling-through of getting to know each other's personalities and interests and needs. And adding to the complexity, John and I were engaged in a similar process with each other. We hoped, then, that our curriculum, classroom organization, and activities would quickly become the focal point of our time together. They would form an ongoing set of *shared* experiences for our diverse group of children and adults to come together in positive and mutually satisfying ways over the school year.

At the close of the morning meeting on the second day of school, John introduced journal writing to the class. While John and I disagreed about the issue of responding to children's journal entries—John favored a written teacher response on the page, while I wanted the entry to be all the children's—we both wanted the children to write and draw anything they wished and to do so in their own beginning spellings. We also wanted children to talk and interact as they wrote and drew, believing that opportunities to socialize enhanced the academic quality of the journal activity.

Because we hadn't discussed the specific journal procedures beforehand, Belva and I listened along with the children as John introduced journal writing to the class.

"Boys and girls," John said, holding a booklet of writing paper covered with red construction paper, "this is called a journal. Mr. Meier and I made a big pile of them. Each has a cover and there's space inside for you to write and draw. We'll start journals today. When you get to your table, the first thing you need to do is write your name on the cover and also write the number 1 and draw a circle around it. This will be your first journal."

John pointed to the example in his hand.

"The next thing to do on the cover is copy down 'My Journal' on the cover. See, 'My Journal' is here on the board. Once you've done that, open your journal. It opens this way, just like a book. You can write and draw about *anything* you want in your journal: what you like to do, your favorite television show, your pets, your favorite games, anything. At the end of the year, you'll have a lot of journals to take home! The pictures that you'll draw go in the picture space at the top of the page. Your writing, your letters and words, will go on these writing lines at the bottom. If you don't know how to spell, don't worry. Just put down as many letters as you can, and it's fine if you ask other kids how to spell or draw. We'll help you, too. When you're done with your journal, raise your hand and we'll respond by writing and talking with you."

John and I envisioned journal writing as a central language arts activity for promoting a beginning understanding of sound–letter correspondences and the notion that a written text has a message and a meaning. We also wanted students to use their own "invented" spelling, to spell according to the letters and letter sounds they knew, in order to foster fluidity and creativity in their writing. John and I also knew from experience that this more open-ended emphasis on spelling would free us to spend more time on the content of children's writing, rather than answering a steady stream of "how do I spell ___?" questions from the children.

John and I also wanted our students to interact with their neighbors by discussing the content of their journals, asking each other for assistance, and generally enjoying themselves as they worked. We also designed the activity to promote one-to-one teacher–student interaction by responding both verbally and in writing to the children's entries when they were "done" or "finished" (signaled by a raised hand and an "I'm ready for you to respond."). Last, the journals would serve as year-long records of the children's literacy learning for the children and their families to see their growth, and for John and me to assess informally the children's writing development. John showed me a useful journal assessment sheet he had designed, and we decided to use it three or four times over the course of the year to document the children's learning.

After John's instructions to the class, he dismissed the children by groups to their tables, where the children readied their red journals and selected thick blue pencils and fat Crayola crayons from the tubs. Crayon mark by crayon mark, pencil scrawl by pencil scrawl, the children embarked on their first reading and writing work of their first grade experience. John and I looked at each other and smiled as the children got down to work; we had had little idea how the activity would go over, but it was working. The children "got" what the activity was about, and the energy and enthusiasm of the moment defined our shared teaching interests in helping children explore and learn about the written and drawn page.

During the journal writing session, the children approached the common task according to their individual talents and interests. What followed showed us the diverse ways in which our particular group of children interpreted a shared academic task, our directions, the social life of their new peers, and interactions with their two new teachers.

Seated at the table by the windows, firmly holding a big blue pencil in his left hand, Dwight first drew a rectangular structure with two small squares resembling windows. He then scribbled in a sky and a sun to the right and left, its rays looking like the outstretched arms of a starfish. In the foreground, Dwight added a stick person with arms, no hands, and a thick line around his head like a helmet. Farther back and in the center, Dwight drew a cylindrical object with a round top that stood taller than the human figure. Dwight completed his picture by adding flowers and grass along the bottom.

He wrote "SSUP" as his text. Dwight translated the caption to John as, "This is an astronaut."

John responded by writing, "Do you want to be an astronaut?" at the bottom of the page.

Dwight nodded.

Sensing Dwight's interest in writing more, John gently clasped his hand over Dwight's, and helped him form the letters for "Y-E-S." Dwight smiled, proud of his first work of the new school year.

Jerome, sitting on the other side of the classroom from Dwight, wore a red t-shirt, red nylon sweat pants, and a light multicolored windbreaker. His Raiders cap from the first day of school had been left at home, and we could see that Jerome's black hair was cut short. Jerome pulled back the cover of his journal. I leaned over to help him make a crease. Picking up a pencil with his right hand, Jerome began drawing a sun, a stick figure to the left, another figure inside a box that looked like a television, and a row of flowers along the bottom. Facing the empty writing lines, I sensed Jerome's hesitation in making the "representational leap" onto the page.

"Do you need any help, Jerome?"

Up went his big eyelashes, and he shyly glanced left and right to see if anyone was listening.

"I don't know how to write."

"That's okay. What do you want it to say?"

"My grandmother."

"Okay. What do you hear at the beginning of 'my'?"

"M?"

"Good. M."

Jerome pursed his lips and wrote an "M" with great concentration. He looked up and I smiled. Jerome grinned and glanced at his neighbors.

Across the table, Carl picked up on Jerome's look. Good-naturedly, he stopped working and asked if Jerome needed any help. Jerome nodded ever so slightly, and I slipped away.

Sometimes sensing when to slip away and let other children teach is as important as knowing when to stay and help.

"I'm trying to write 'my grandmother,'" Jerome said.

Carl took over by helping Jerome write "MYGRnDNrMTh" as his text. When Jerome eventually raised his hand, Belva walked over.

"I love your picture. What does your writing say, Jerome?" she asked.

"I love my grandmother."

"I'm glad for you," Belva said. "That's a nice thing to feel."

Interpreting John's notion of "responding" to the children's journals in her own way, Belva wrote Jerome's verbatim "I love my grandmother" rather than her own reaction. Jerome was pleased.

Carl returned to his journal and drew Freddie Krueger (star character of the horror movie *Nightmare on Elm Street*) zooming across the page in a spaceship. Carefully rendered in mixed colors, the spaceship resembled a small Chitty Chitty Bang Bang contraption with exhaust spewing from an extensive tailpipe. Freddie Krueger, with arms out to the side, sat astride the ship as it flew. Carl described the picture by writing "VDE gR gSqAD CECE q."

Carl interpreted his writing for Belva as "Freddie Krueger flies in space," which Belva wrote down for him. Then, obviously not knowing Freddie Krueger's identity, Belva added her own response: "Gee! I would like to fly with him." She read her response back to Carl, who gave her a bit of a double-look.

At the end of the same table, Nicole quietly went about her journal work. A tall girl with a big broad smile, her black hair tied into two long thick pigtails, Nicole used swift, bold strokes to fill in the entire drawing space. Nicole neatly placed the lid under the bottom of the crayon box, and carefully exchanged one color at a time. She first suspended a bright sun just below the top of the page, floated a fluffy cloud to the right, created a house with front steps and a potted plant sitting in a curtained window, and drew a healthy and upright row of flowers in the foreground. For her text, Nicole wrote "Th IRIOEE Magaaoeey LAeeORR."

When Nicole shyly raised her hand, John approached and knelt beside her, placing one arm on the end of the table.

"What does your journal say?"

"The girl is playing outside."

As Nicole listened and watched, John slowly read aloud as he wrote, "What is the little girl's name?" below Nicole's writing.

Nicole shook her head and leaned on one of her hands; she didn't want to reveal the girl's identity.

On the other side of Nicole's table, Gina continued the suddenly popular sun drawing. Allowing the children to select their own topics as we did, rather than setting one theme or topic for all the children, already encouraged the children's sharing and "migration of ideas" around the children's group tables.

Gina, her black pigtails braided tightly with red clips on the bottom and green barrettes on top, drew a sliver of a sun in the upper right corner of her page showering light on two figures walking along a street. A girl with long flowing hair crowned with a big bow entered from the left, and walked with arms akimbo toward the center. The girl's dress had three dots for buttons and a small square for a pocket. On the other side of the road, a boy with the number 32 emblazoned on his chest and the letter "B" on his tall hat walked toward her. Gina penned the date, minus the year, on the first line. Line one of her text read "Was T Ga," "BodcL.TCALI" on line 2, "LdanbF /////" on line 3, "Co Too soI Love you" on line 4, and "ILgooGoLcLLdq" on the last.

Antonia, working alongside Gina, created a similar entry. Antonia drew a rainbow and a girl with her hair done up in ribbons and outfitted in a triangular dress. Antonia's text was almost identical to Gina's: "Wasl" on line 1, "Bodcl.TCALI" on line 2, "LdAabF///////" on line 3, and "Coloos.I Love you" on line 4. The two girls weren't so much copying each other, though they were doing that on paper, as doing the journal activity in the same way in order to promote their budding friendship.

At the next table, Eugene, his Medusa-like curls almost falling over his glasses, drew a fiery scene of thick red, black, and brown crayon markings. He softened the scene by adding a bright yellow five-pointed sun with a smiling face on the side. Eugene's caption helped explain the picture: "THeSTRFRiYei-ThEFGiTBG" on line 1 and "BGBGBG" on line 2. Using the most essential letters, "STR" stood for story, "FR" stood for "fire" and "BG" for "big." Eugene saw little need for vowels, "FR" more efficiently resembling "fire" than "FI" or "IR" or "ER." He relied on consonants and left the vowels implied.

"How did his house start on fire?" John wrote in response.

Like Nicole, Eugene shyly shook his head and didn't answer; he didn't want to respond. John just smiled and put a reassuring hand on his shoulder.

Edward, a thin boy with his black hair shaved close, took several long minutes to write his name and copy "My Journal" from the chalkboard onto his cover. For the date, he wrote "Septemp." For his drawing, Edward drew a large cage-like object with several vertical lines. He ran out of time for a text. Edward had a physical disability that made forming letters and shapes difficult, and writing required concentration and effort. Edward would soon receive physical therapy to strengthen his walking and running (he wore plastic ankle braces under his trousers) and occupational therapy for fine-motor skills such as drawing, writing, and cutting. John and I immediately admired Edward's determination in manipulating the big blue pencil, and decided for the time being to help him as he wished.

Next to Edward, Arthur filled his first journal page with pencil and crayon abstractions. It was six-year-old Picasso. In the text space, Arthur wrote "FlCSRICbOlSB" on line 1 in pencil, "September" on line 2 in crayon, and "bab9TOnT3hOi" on line 3 in pencil.

Arthur put a shy fist into the air and leaned back in his chair. John walked over and Arthur interpreted his writing as "This is a big fire."

John wrote, "When I see a fire, I'll call the fireman!"

Still leaning back, Arthur folded his arms across his Hawaiian-style cotton shirt, buttoned nearly to the top over a white t-shirt, and smiled.

Arthur's other neighbor, Maria, continued the sun theme made popular by the girls. She drew a yellow circle at the top of the picture space and two troll-like figures on either side. Maria, her dark brown hair pulled into a neat ponytail at the top of her head, worked quietly. After creating the sun, Maria added four lines rising above the head of a person on the left, and one long line, hooking back slightly at the end, extending to another figure. A small duck-like animal stood above the foreground shaded in with heavy crayon. Maria wrote "WSCUR" as her text.

With Belva at her side, adjusting her reading glasses on the string around her neck, Maria softly offered a translation, "I went to the park with my sister," which Belva wrote down with a knowing smile.

Across the room at the "red triangle" table, unbeknownst to Dwight, Joshua carried on the boys' intrigue with space like a budding six-year-old science fiction writer. Joshua's large spaceship, rounded at the front, had four triangular wings and a rectangular tail and moved across the page with speed. Using bold, strong crayon strokes like Nicole, Joshua drew a circle and a quartet of four-pointed stars encircling the ship. The background between the shapes and the ship was colored black. For a text, Joshua wrote, "TH IS THE HRi HA SAS HP."

Joshua, like the other children, wasn't so much drawing and writing—though he was—as creating and forming an imaginary-real world in the moment. Our "job," then, as teachers was to see and respond to this interest and motivation of the children, as well as to their attempts at representing themselves on paper.

Belva happened by and asked Joshua about his work.

"Oh, this is a spaceship," Joshua explained matter-of-factly. "It's a hammerhead spaceship. You see, there are four wings and it can fly at high altitude and really fast."

Belva responded by writing, "Joshua, I like your hammerhead spaceship. You drew a great picture."

At the other end of the table, Joey and Warren pulled their chairs side by side. On the second day of school, the two tall, wiry boys already enjoyed working together. Joey drew six thick vertical lines in crayon and behind the lines sketched a pollywog-like figure, all arms, legs, and head. He added two four-wheeled objects to the side. Joey wrote "SeptembR11" on the first line and "GENHEN GENHEN" on the second. He interpreted this for Belva as, "This is a jail." Belva shook her head and wrote, "I am afraid of jails. Are you?" In a show of first-grade bravado, with Warren as his audience of one, Joey shook his head. (Later in the fall, we learned that Joey's mother worked at the county jail.)

Warren also worked on the jail theme, creating a large rectangle with a dozen vertical lines in the middle. He wrote "JAL" for a caption and read it to John as "jail."

John slowly wrote, "Have you ever seen a real jail?"

With Joey present, Warren started a slow nod, but changed to a shake of the head when John gave him a raised eyebrow.

Seated next to Warren and Joey, Deborah paid no attention to the boys' fascination with jails. A tall girl, her brown cheeks dimpling as she smiled, Deborah drew a girl with an extra-large head tilted to the right, causing the girl's long hair and eyes to fall in the same direction. The girl's body was razor thin, her arms tiny and short. A half-circle served as the nose. Her lips were big and rosy. Deborah wrote "W N i To ThePrtee—ing" underneath.

She translated her writing as, "When I went to the birthday party I had fun."

I wrote, "Whose birthday party was it?"

Deborah picked up her pencil and, taking me by surprise, took the initiative to respond to *my* response. She wrote "Joseee."

"She's my best friend," Deborah explained.

Mothers and grandmothers, astronauts and hammerhead spaceships, monsters and jails, flowers and suns, fires, farms, parties, and Freddie Krueger. These were the themes our students presented in their first journal work of the year. As they worked and socialized, the children revealed a diversity of styles, interests, abilities, and temperaments—Michael became confused and wrote "My Journal" on the inside page rather than the cover, Nicole colored in her entire page, Joshua created a hammerhead spaceship, Carl helped Jerome write "my grandmother," and Antonia and Gina created nearly identical texts.

As with any new class of students at the start of the school year, John and I didn't know what would unfold. On the second day of school, we had set a common task for the class with the journals, common in materials, goal, method, and instructions, and yet once under way and in motion, the children differentiated themselves through their individual ways of engaging in the activity and their desire to feel successful socially and academically.

In the first hour's worth of working and social interaction of the new school year, John and I gleaned important details about our class and how we worked together as a beginning classroom community. Based on their interactions and journal work, the children enjoyed the activity and found their own comfortable toeholds within the parameters we set and the particular personalities in our room. Along the way, those who enjoyed and felt comfortable drawing, drew. Those who felt competent and wanted to write, wrote. Those who liked to talk and socialize as they worked, did.

Through an important focus of our first-grade curriculum, journal writing and drawing, John and I were pleased to make early inroads in getting to know our students and promoting a climate of cooperation and interest in each other. We were also glad to see the children's active involvement in the journals—from the sun theme to Deborah's written response to my response to Carl's helping Jerome write. These and other instances revealed the benefits of our giving over a certain measure of control to the children. By encouraging student choice of writing topics and drawing, and promoting opportunities to talk and socialize, John and I relinquished a measure of our traditional teacher authority and power. But in doing so, we wanted the children to meet us halfway; we hoped they would bring their interests and engagement to the task, making connections to the journals, each other, John and me, and themselves. John and I were glad to see early evidence of this process, a hoped-for cornerstone of our shared classroom.

We very much wanted the children's work to "grow directly out of the unique local situation" we set in motion on the first day of school. John and I wanted the "unique personalities" of our classroom, as well as the "social context" of talking and interacting around the journals, to guide the children's entrance into our classroom world.

Pleased with the first day of journal writing, and thinking it would provide a calm and engaging beginning to each school day, John and I put it in the leadoff position in our daily schedule.

4

Rhythm–
The Art of Classroom Discipline

I can ACnQ

I can not BPP PQA

I can be nice. I cannot punch.

by Nicole

*But when the animation in a large class is so strong that it
interferes with a teacher in his attempt to guide the class,
then one feels tempted to cry out against the children and to
subdue that spirit. If that animation has the lesson for an object,
then nothing better is to be desired. But if the animation has
passed over to another object, the fault is with the teacher who
did not manage that animation properly.*

Tolstoy, *On Education*

For new and experienced teachers alike, classroom discipline is not an isolated program or set of techniques separate from the life of a classroom. Rather, as John and I learned anew, creating a calm and stable teaching and learning environment is an art that extends to sensitive and powerful aspects of classroom and school life. Although John and I didn't know it at the beginning of the year, this would become a year-long challenge.

As John hinted, by the second week of school we gained six more students—Roger, Ernesto, Robert, Kimberly, Keith, and Galen. And the children's honeymoon period of good behavior quickly ended. In September, and on into the fall, John and I struggled to create an underlying sense of stability and order in our classroom. Without this foundation, the children couldn't settle into any kind of rhythm in their learning and John and I couldn't hit our stride in our teaching.

Discipline problems and a lack of order in classrooms are sometimes attributed to differences of life experience, culture, and educational background among teachers, students, and their families. In our shared teaching journal and in person, John and I discussed at length how our classroom's diversity may or may not have influenced classroom order and the overall state of human relationships. While we reached no easy answers, it was important to address the issue together as co-teachers early in the year, and to continue sorting out the complicated mix of factors influencing our particular classroom.

John and I discussed the fact that we had 19 boys and 8 girls. This gender imbalance placed an extra challenge on our efforts to create a calm and orderly classroom. In terms of the children's peer relations and friendships, for each boy there were 18 other boys to choose from as potential friends. For each girl, there were only 7 girls to serve as potential friends. Although our numerical imbalance made for some difficulty in making friends of the same gender, it did encourage certain boys and girls to cross over gender boundaries and make friends with each other. Over the course of the year, we had a few strong boy–girl friendships.

Personally and professionally, John and I were frustrated with ourselves as we worked to promote a calm and predictable classroom environment. We knew what success in this area felt like from our previous teaching assignments, and we expected the same in our new situation. John and I had both left our most long-standing teaching positions on a high note, well liked by the children, families, administration, and community members. Starting in September, and on into the fall, John and I felt like we were learning how to teach all over again. We also hoped that our new colleagues, Marian, and our children's parents wouldn't catch on to us and notice the lack of underlying order.

John and I also felt a certain source of embarrassment that we weren't doing better, that our classroom wasn't as orderly and smoothly running as we "knew" it could be. John, who took a great interest and teaching pride in maintaining classroom order, was particularly bothered by our challenges in creating a stable classroom. When John taught in Arizona, he told me, he could leave his classroom of students and return to a quiet and calm room. And whatever he said to the children, they listened and followed directions—he was the "maestro."

Although John and I couldn't see it at the time, for we were too mired in the instability of our classroom, a little humor and a sense of perspective would have helped ease our frustration. John and I needed to remind ourselves, with a laugh here and there, of the enduring capacity and the ever-present smarts of six-year-olds to derail and foil adult intentions and plans.

As John and I learned, it is in teachers' proactive and reactive efforts to the inevitable compounding of little scenes and incidents, enacted over and over again, that an overall sense of order in a classroom is both created and maintained. And the real danger comes when teachers waver or lose perspective and the gates open a little, things get chaotic, and feelings of confidence and control are replaced by feelings of helplessness and frustration.

Our shared teaching journal and the journal I kept at home helped us relive and reconstruct our too-often anguished attempts at creating sheer classroom order. Belying the calm and meditative swirling of its Italian-marbled cover, our journal recorded our feelings of frustration, disappointment, and even anger . . .

Monday, 17 September (John)
    Quite a frustrating day. I guess it is the "Monday Phenomenon" and the clock not working. Read the rest of *Fish Is Fish* and the activity took all afternoon because of the students not listening to directions. We did *no* math.

Tuesday, 18 September (John)

I'm fried! I got so upset with Dwight today I put him near our desk (you can change it if you want) and he did wonderfully! He finished his work and was happy with it!

Wednesday, 19 September (Daniel)

Great AM, bad PM! That whole lunch thing and the transition into the afternoon throws too many of them off. Difficulties: 1. Dwight 2. Joey 3. Edward 4. Carl 5. Robert (better) Rug area still a problem—should we assign seats?

Thursday, 20 September (Daniel)

Belva read *Inch by Inch* today. Belva was great!! We then did a page or two of the book I made up on *Inch by Inch* and I'll hopefully finish it by Friday. Please do a page if you wish. Handwriting took too long—let's do two rows?! I had them * or + their "best first grade letter" after each row was done!

Friday, 21 September (Daniel)

"Friday Madness!" Seating continues to be a problem—Robert and Amanda are not good together. She had a hard day and I will call her mom tonight. Edward and Michele also had difficulties. So did Joey. The new child, Keith, almost hit Carl, he got so mad at him. We've got to change the seating at the tables—I already switched Nicole and Michael. Should we get more tables?

John and I intended the journal as a place to exchange information on the class; we never thought it would become a safe place for venting and sharing our frustrations with discipline problems.

The journal helped us take a step back, move away from the intensity of our interactions with the children and their interactions with each other. The journal writing slowed down an incident or scene, helping us tease apart possible underlying reasons and factors. Often in teaching, and especially when there is little time and space afforded for thinking and reflecting, what appears at first glance as a neatly packaged discipline problem doesn't get at other reasons for an unhappy child or particular ongoing struggles between teachers and students. "Disruptive" and "behavior problems," then, become shortcut and handy code words for far more complicated issues.

But with 27 students, an energetic class, and the new experience of co-teaching, like many other teachers John and I had little time and energy to overturn every incident in searching for underlying reasons for our classroom discipline problems. We were doing our best to stay a step ahead of the class, first reacting and then trying to understand difficult situations as they arose.

As happens to teachers and others who work with large groups of children, maintaining order can border on an obsession. In September and October, crucial months for establishing a sense of rhythm in a classroom, John and I too often found ourselves fretting over incidents and scenes of misbehavior. This focus only served to distract us from our biggest goal—common, whole-class engagement with the academic content of our first grade curriculum. And like rows of stacked dominoes, which only get knocked over again each time they're reset, our overemphasis on classroom control encouraged our growing perception that "the problem" resided in several of the same children.

John and I couldn't help the unstated thought, "Why can't our students just come to school ready to learn?" It would be so much easier, we reasoned, if the children "knew" how to sit still at morning meeting, follow directions, make the transition from one activity to another, and get along with peers without fighting or arguing. In thinking along these lines, John and I naturally and unwittingly fell into an "us against them" syndrome that didn't stop the cycle of interactional and discipline difficulties.

Back in late August, John and I had briefly discussed a classroom discipline program. John suggested using a "stop light" discipline chart. In this system, children start the day under the "green light," designated on the chart with a green circle; if children misbehave, their names move to "yellow"; if they misbehave again they move to "orange" and then finally to "red." At each light, appropriate punishments are meted out: a time out away from the group, loss of recess, phone call home to parents.

At my private school, I didn't use a prescribed discipline system. Sizing up each situation, I either talked directly with the children about the incident, put the children on time-out, sent the misbehaving students to the principal, or talked with their parents. In general, I tried to promote a calm and orderly classroom based on the quality of my personal interactions with the children, believing that my personality and beliefs about proper social behavior would win out.

I told John that while we needed to agree on a common set of discipline expectations and consequences, the stop light system seemed too public and too focused on negative behavior; I thought it would only embarrass and label certain individual children as troublemakers. Unable to agree on a common discipline program, John and I compromised and decided to work on behavior problems in ways we each considered effective and successful.

As discipline issues arose in our classroom, John and I implemented activities and "management techniques" to promote a better sense of responsibility, respect, and cooperation among the children. In September, John worked with the children on a Rule Book based on the class rules from the first day of school.

1. Play fair.
2. Do not damage anything.
3. Take turns talking.
4. Keep your hands and feet to yourself.
5. Don't hurt other people's feelings.

Each of the five sheets was divided into an "I can _____" and an "I cannot _____" section.

For "Do not damage anything," Joshua drew himself cheerfully walking in the grass and extending his leg, indicated with an arrow, to kick someone. He wrote "NoKkg" (no kicking) below.

For "Play fair," Kimberly drew herself playing on the bars outside and wrote "PL" (I can play). She also drew a girl hitting another girl, complete with a vertical row of colored lines showing the effect of the bop on the head. Underneath, Kimberly wrote "HSTT" (I cannot hit).

Ernesto, newly arrived from South America, copied enough of "I can" to write "I CANTAC," and carefully drew a television set, a church with a blue cross on top, and a foot kicking a soccer ball. Ernesto wrote "I CANNOT" for "I cannot," and drew himself throwing a hammer at a tree and holding a slingshot, and a car hitting a small stick figure.

In late September, John informed me in our shared journal that he was handing out three stickers to students "when they do things right, like lining up, reading silently, etc.," and found "that it seems to help." For "minor infractions," John put their names on the chalkboard and took away five minutes of recess.

I didn't try the sticker idea because it seemed like a stop-gap approach only good for three children at a time. I did try the classic name-on-the-board trick, though, but when the list of names grew to double digits, both the children and I sensed the folly of this tactic. I also made the mistake of having misbehaving children lose entire recesses over relatively small misdeeds, leaving me without more severe consequences for more serious misbehavior. As I furiously wrote down several children's names on the chalkboard, bellowing, "All right, all of you will miss recess," I undermined my own effectiveness; the list was public evidence of the high number of misbehaving children, and my bellowing only revealed my lack of patience and level of exasperation.

When I then trotted the half-dozen or more "in trouble" children outside to the playground bench, they only ended up playing and fooling around on the benches. If I kept them inside in the classroom, I had to watch them and I didn't get a break. In both instances, I actually increased the difficulty of the situation by dragging it out for both the children and myself. The discipline and interactional difficulties wore us down, involving almost daily incidents in which the children and John and I didn't want to give in and lose face in public. This only led to a standoff, both sides using their leverage to stand their ground. It didn't make for enjoyable and fruitful teaching and learning.

Too often, instead of working with the entire class, John and I concentrated on stopping individual children from misbehaving. And in trying to prevent small brush fires from becoming a full-blown firestorm, we actually increased the chances; running from small fire to small fire with a tiny watering can didn't bring the entire situation under control—a sustained, powerful burst of water was needed.

After lunch on a hot October day, I took the class outside for P.E. I had the children sit in a circle on the grass. Before I could announce the first game, Amanda and Carl and Michele complained of the heat and wanted to sit under the shady trees. I said no, and not wanting a critical mass of others to defect, I stood my ground and repeated my directive for them to sit on the grass. They reluctantly complied.

In our warm-up game, we passed the ball around the circle as fast as we could. The children loved it and spontaneously called it "Hot Potato," moving the red rubber ball faster and faster around the circle until Edward and a few other boys started throwing the ball at their neighbors. They were enjoying the new game, but I wasn't amused and sensed the game might fall apart. Singling out Edward as the ringleader, I told him to sit out of the circle for throwing the ball. Edward protested, pointing out that others also threw the ball. He was right, but I felt that I had to restore order. Edward gave me a pout-stare and slowly moved into the shade.

We played Duck Duck Goose next. The children loved patting each other's heads, running around the circle, yelling, and finally plopping down at the vacated spot. After a few go-rounds, though, Amanda lost interest and, bothered by the heat, refused to play. Again worried that others would follow, I curtly told Amanda she could just sit out for the rest of the time. I then felt bad about snapping at Amanda, and told Edward he could rejoin us; somehow I thought this would even things out. He refused. At this point, what seemed like a fun time in the sun playing games was degenerating into a discipline problem. I was frustrated, not to mention hot myself. But I continued the game. Arthur scooted around the now lopsided circle to catch Steven. As I watched the race, joining the cheering children, I heard someone crying. I looked around the circle and saw Deborah holding her left arm below the shoulder. Huge tears streamed down her hot, brown face. The children stopped and looked at Deborah.

"Deborah, what's the matter?" I asked.

Between convulsive sobbing she blurted out, "A bee! A bee stung me!"

I envisioned Deborah dying on the spot should she be allergic and never stung before. I took Deborah by the arm, ordered the children to follow, and led the class to the office. I parked the class in the hallway and rushed Deborah into the office. Cindy checked Deborah's emergency card. Deborah wasn't allergic. The good news didn't quiet Deborah, and we returned to the classroom with the still-sobbing Deborah ahead of 26 hot, sweaty, and cranky children.

After letting myself get thrown off by a hot potato game gone awry and the bee scare, the rest of the afternoon went downhill. Instead of laughing off the incident as one of those unexpected flops in teaching young children, I lost a sense of what was needed to regroup the children and myself. Instead of pulling the class together upstairs on the rug with a calming activity or game, I had them get back to work at their tables. Keith reported that Carl took his pencil; Robert got out of his seat, wouldn't listen to me, and didn't complete any tasks; at story time, several boys sat in a self-styled "boys club" on the rug and excluded the rest of the boys and all the girls.

Although they didn't deserve it, I announced "free choice time" at the end of the day; I hoped it would bring a peaceful end to the day. It didn't. Steven told Joshua that he was taking all the "good" pattern blocks, and then Steven tried to grab some back. I then asked Steven to leave the rug area. He didn't want to and cried. Meanwhile, Joey and Arthur and Robert peacefully snapped Lego pieces into planes and trucks and houses until Keith noticed that Joey had more green rectangles, good for building. Like a halfback diving for a touchdown, Keith lunged for Joey's stack and the two boys rolled around on the rug until I peeled them apart. By 2:20, when the day finally ended, I was exhausted.

Other incidents and interactions took on larger-than-life proportions because they kept touching our fear of losing total control of our class.

Even something as apparently innocuous as managing the supply of pencils, erasers, and markers proved mettlesome. By the end of September, the small eight-crayon cardboard boxes were torn and ripped and children complained of a box not having "a red" or "two oranges and no black." This prompted some children to make their own search-and-find missions to other tables, this surreptitious crayon hunting resembling a game of Capture the Flag.

To an outsider, our crayon problem may seem funny and trivial. But for us, the crayons were yet another source of frustration and evidence of our general lack of classroom order. One day John threw away the crayon boxes and placed large handfuls of loose crayons into the tubs; he had had enough. But this only changed the locus of the problem; without individual boxes of crayons, all the children at a table only had access to one tub. Enterprising table group members then tried to seize sole possession of the tub, doling out crayons as they pleased, or more than one child made a simultaneous grab for the tub and argued over who got it first.

In the ensuing Great Crayon Hunt, some students hoarded favorite colors or single reds or blues or blacks, stashing them inside journals and cubbies. By mid-October, most crayons were broken and chewed, and any full-size crayons were highly sought after. One day, when I innocently emptied a few boxes of brand-new crayons into the most crayon-depleted tub, the rumor spread of their arrival and attempts were made to hijack the new crayons for private use. Finally, John and I arrived at a rather simple solution: we added new crayons to *all* the tubs at the same time.

The pencils caused an additional headache. So many children liked to sharpen their pencils that a seemingly perpetual line formed at the sharpener. Children tried to cut the line, the sharpener made a lot of noise, pencils got stuck and broke, and the pencil shavings overflowed onto the floor. So John and I finally instituted a new rule that only teachers could sharpen pencils. But like the crayon dilemma, this only brought up a new quandary. As the pencils became chewed, gnawed, and shortened even after new ones were issued, some children searched other group tubs for the longest pencils and the most intact erasers. These pencils became a hot commodity. If a child left for the bathroom, another child might make off with the departed student's pencil, which led to cries of "He took my pencil!" At the time, John and I couldn't see any magical solution, and took a wait-and-see attitude on the "pencil problem."

In trying to alleviate our discipline difficulties, John and I relied more and more on the built-in strength of our teaching partnership. Our shared journal continued to provide a place for observations and reflections.

2 October (Daniel)
Annoyed that most of the children were not cleaning up well last Thursday, I got extra mad at Dwight. I shouldn't have taken it out on him. But I did. He started to cry. I said I was sorry and that I didn't mean to get so mad at him. It didn't seem to help. He kept on crying. It was at that moment that I realized that Dwight was a small, vulnerable child and not the tough kid that I often thought of. I felt bad for him, myself, the whole situation. The next day Dwight came in early, before the rest of the children, to feed Foo Foo. I was glad to see him.

9 October (John)
I had some dreams about Robert, Keith, and Dwight. Those poor children. I have to deal with them better. I just don't know how. I use to think I was an excellent teacher, but if I let 3–4 slip through the cracks I can't claim "excellence." I sit them outside; I reach the point where I just don't care, as long as they are not

disrupting the class! Really! There are all these other needy children in the room.

16 October (John)
     Yesterday morning wasn't too bad. Generally, Mondays continue to be tough. I did a few writing conferences with the children which went well except most students are not really writing anything. I think the conferences will get better as we have more of them. We also need to devise a way to "record" what happens in the conferences. I attempted a notation sheet–rather crude. The afternoon was terrible. Thank God for Maria [university tutor]. The class did eventually start to work cooperatively after forty-five minutes of hell. Then it lasted about five to ten minutes. But they did it! Don't quote me on this but . . . maybe we should use the basal math book?! I looked at them . . . what a waste of money. It's almost not worth the "busy work."

19 October (Daniel)
     I asked Janet what she does when things get loud in the class. She said, "I cover my ears!" Isn't that something?!

John and I were thankful for this ongoing opportunity to share and communicate our teaching troubles—it helped us feel less alone and more like a unified partnership.

One of our most perplexing obstacles to promoting a stable learning environment involved interactional difficulties between the children themselves. These disputes were rooted in children's individual issues and in the overarching tenor and mood of our classroom.

Amanda had a difficult beginning of the year. She was easily provoked into getting angry at other children, which often resulted in pushing tables and yelling. Just before 2:20 in early October, Edward called Amanda a name. Then someone pushed Amanda's table. Amanda pulled the table way back, picked the end up, and yelled, "Stop pushing the table." Amanda's tablemates yelled back. I moved toward Amanda to calm her.

At this point, with the classroom door open and parents waiting outside in the hallway, Dwight decided to join in. He made some funny faces at Amanda, they called each other names, and Amanda yelled more loudly for Dwight to "be quiet before I come over to you." Luckily the bell rang, and without leaving Amanda's side, I told the class they could leave. Amanda and Dwight continued to argue across the room until Amanda started to cry. Edward made his way, ever so slowly, to his cubby to get his stuff, looking at Amanda as he went. Amanda, still crying, made a move toward Edward, but I gently pulled Amanda back.

Mrs. Brown, Joey's mother, then appeared with another parent. Embarrassed at the end-of-the-day chaos, and immobile as I remained with Amanda, I asked Mrs. Brown if she could help Edward get on his way. No problem, she said, and escorted Edward out the door. After I told Amanda that things would be all right and tomorrow would be a new day, she nodded and stopped crying.

In an underlying story line, Joey and Amanda had been carrying on a mini-feud for the previous week or two, arguing and taunting each other over apparently minor things.

25 September (John)
      I talked with Mrs. Moore [Amanda's mother] about this week and last's behavior problems. I also received a visit from Mrs. Brown. She said Amanda bothered Joey all day yesterday. "He complained all night about it," she said. She was upset. She wanted to talk with Amanda so Amanda would leave Joey alone. I convinced her to give us two weeks and if things haven't changed, she could talk with Marian. She agreed. I watched them and it was *Joey* that was bothering Amanda. So I talked with him!

The next morning, as we worked in our journals, Joey arrived late with Mrs. Brown. He carried two tall white daisies wrapped in a wet paper towel and tinfoil. As the class looked on, Joey handed the flowers to Amanda.

"I'm sorry," Joey said.

"He picked them himself from our garden," Mrs. Brown said to me. "It was his idea."

I helped Amanda put the flowers in a cup of water by the sink. Later that day, Amanda typed me a letter on the typewriter in the writing center: "dea dan, i like too be in your clas. do you like it id do I love too be in your do you I do do you lovee to." Feeling better about her relationship with Joey, Amanda felt more connected with me and the class.

As happens with teachers new to a school and unfamiliar with families and the community, John and I only found out later the reasons for some of Amanda and Joey's difficulties. It was not until the middle of October, during our once-a-year parent conference, that we learned from Mrs. Moore, Amanda's mother, that Amanda's grandmother had suddenly died just before the beginning of school. The grandmother had lived with them, and she and Amanda were particularly close; Amanda was taking the death quite hard. This important piece of information helped us place Amanda's behavior in perspective, and we were able to be more empathetic and understanding of Amanda's classroom outbursts.

Through Jodi, a kindergarten colleague who had taught Joey the year before, we later learned that Mrs. Brown worked nights at the county jail, slept during the day, and wasn't always able to monitor Joey's bedtime or help him get organized in the morning. His older sister had these responsibilities. This information provided a larger backdrop for looking at Joey's in-class difficulties with paying attention and getting along with others.

And yet no amount of knowledge, and no single discipline technique or program, would have prevented all our interactional problems. So along the way, John and I learned some hard lessons about the ins and outs of promoting and maintaining classroom order.

One particularly persistent challenge involved a battle of wills in which John and I confronted individual students head on, which quickly degenerated into a show of teacher power and authority versus the children's wily abilities to derail us. In an important lesson, and one we kept relearning over the course of the school year, John and I learned that a public display of teacher power is sometimes necessary (some students expect and rely on it) to establish ourselves as in control and accomplish our teacherly agenda.

Yet we also learned, as I experienced with Amanda and Edward in the games, to allow students to save face and avoid embarrassment in front of their peers and their teachers. It gives children an honorable way out, and a chance to retain their identity as part of the group. Too often, as John and I also learned, teachers feel that students are giving them a hard time, when the children in question are actually playing to their peers. In the "kid culture" of a classroom, what can be termed "misbehavior," and is given that continued emphasis, can become a currency for children to bond together out of their desire for peer friendships. This then made for a tricky pattern of misperceiving certain kinds of actions and language that, as teachers, John and I needed to manipulate and redirect. And we found that this would take time.

On a Sunday in October, John and I met for a cafe latte. After sipping the chocolate powder off the top, we talked about our frustrations with our classroom. We needed more order. John suggested implementing activity or learning centers, which had worked well for him in Arizona. I was ready to try almost anything at this point, even something like centers, which I had never used before. So I agreed. John and I then discussed possible ways to organize and run activity centers.

1. We could place children in preselected small groups and rotate the children through specific activity centers focused on a variety of curricular areas: math, art, reading, writing, science, social studies. The rotations could come at set time intervals or simply when we decided groups needed to switch.
2. We could put out center activities around the classroom and allow children to select activities of their choice, and limit the number of children at each activity table.
3. As children worked in center groups, we could take one center group at a time until we had worked with all the groups over the course of the morning or day.

4. While groups worked independently at their center activities, we could pull
    out any number of children for one-to-one or small-group instruction as
    we saw fit. Since we had Belva in the mornings, she could also take a small
    group or work with one child.

    After discussing the merits of each option, we decided on a simple ver-
sion to start with in our afternoon math work. Since our next math unit involved
identifying and replicating patterns, John put a variety of math manipulatives
on the tables.

> *October 2 (John)*
> In the afternoon, I put out one math activity: pattern blocks (multi-
> colored triangles, squares, rectangles, diamonds, and hexagons), Unifix
> cubes (multi-colored interlocking plastic pieces), and tiles (multi-colored
> plastic squares), geoboards on the rug (boards with a grid of nails for
> making patterns and designs with multi-colored rubber bands). The
> children made three patterns and then chose their favorite. They copied
> it on a worksheet or pasted shapes on paper for the pattern blocks. It
> was good until clean-up time.

John explained and showed the children how to rotate through the centers.
He grouped the children according to their regular table groups. As the children worked, John circulated around the room commenting on the pattern
work and redirecting behavior as needed. At 10-minute intervals, John stopped
the children's work by clapping his hands and having the children clap the
pattern back. John then directed one group to wait on the rug until the other
three groups moved to their next center.

The next math unit involved sorting and classifying objects and materials. John sent home a letter asking parents to help children bring in a "junk
collection" of math manipulatives. In the next newsletter, we updated parents on our math work.

> Dear Room 201 Families,
> Our most recent math unit involved making patterns. We created
> patterns with shapes, colors, Unifix cubes, pattern blocks, geoboards,
> tiles, each other, our hands, fingers, and legs! We have also been
> looking for shapes in the world around us. Although we will never
> finish with patterns, they form the basis for much of mathematics; we
> will move on to sorting and classifying soon. Keep sending in that
> junk! We will need it for the math program and especially the sorting
> and classifying unit. We still need: small lids (from toothpaste tubes,
> jars, and lids), old keys, bottle caps (dented ones are fine), buttons, pits
> (from various fruits), small rocks, shells, nuts, bolts and screws (old and
> rusty ones are fine).

Just as they produced wadded-up lunch money on the first day of school, the children brought in a steady supply of plastic and metal lids, keys, nuts and bolts, screws, cork, toothpicks, and pieces of wood in their pockets and backpacks and paper bags. The children loved piling up the junk in the back of the room, and John and I liked the successful home–school connection and cooperation.

Activity centers are praised in teachers' initial and ongoing training for their social and educational benefits—centers promote group work and active learning for children—but such essential specifics as timing and grouping in order to fine-tune and particularize center work are rarely discussed at length. John and I also wanted to use centers because our "quieter" children were receiving less of our attention, and we hoped centers would provide a more consistent and equitable way for all our students to receive our attention and instruction.

In our math unit on patterns, as we set out one material per table and rotated children through all the centers, John and I thought things were too rushed and too chaotic. Judging, then, when and how to switch groups proved tricky; John and I had to wait long enough for a majority of children at a certain center to finish and be prepared to move, and yet we couldn't wait too long because some children became bored and restless. We had to find a comfortable balance between our social and academic goals for the children, the clock, and the children's varying levels of engagement.

Another influential factor in getting our new centers to work involved 27 six-year-olds moving at once and not all heeding our oft-repeated mantra to "remember where your *next* center is." And once arriving at their new activity center, some children jockeyed for the first-come-first-served seating and materials, which led to grabbing of materials, poking of neighbors, keys dropping on the hard plastic tables, and yogurt lids flying through the air like mini-Frisbees. John and I persisted with the afternoon centers, though, convinced we would succeed. After two weeks of patient training and practice, the centers slowly began to foster a newfound rhythm in the afternoons.

Meeting for yet another latte treat, John was "jazzed." The centers were giving our afternoons a more stable foundation; the children were more on task, focused; and interactional problems seemed to be decreasing. Buoyed by our progress, John pushed us a step further and made a pitch for establishing literature groups in the mornings.

"I know," he said, "you've never used heterogeneous or mixed-ability groups, but listen. Literature groups are going to be great. We can do it like I did in Arizona. We'll institute centers in the mornings, just like the afternoons, but we'll regroup the kids in small groups balanced according to gender, temperament, ethnicity, and ability. I'm sure this will tighten up our language arts work in the mornings."

When John was taken with a new idea for our classroom, I found his enthusiasm hard to resist. In my previous teaching, I had relied on homogeneous or same-ability reading groups and used varied levels of books and workbooks. John's idea of small groups of mixed abilities was new for me, and would involve a change of both perspective and method. But not wanting to dampen John's excitement and willing to try something new to help our partnership, I agreed to give literature groups a try. John and I ordered another round of lattes in celebration, and pulled out a class list to form four heterogeneous groups.

John explained the new groupings to the children the next day. He then asked each group to meet together and discuss and vote on a group name. Rap groups, rock-and-roll groups, television characters, fast food restaurants, stuffed animals, movie characters, and actors were bandied about across the tables as possible group names. The naming process took two days, but the children finally came to a consensus on four names. I typed up the groups and then taped the list on the horseshoe table:

M.C. Hammers:	*San Francisco 49ers:*
1. Amanda	1. Joshua
2. Nicole	2. Joey
3. Steven	3. Robert
4. Arthur	4. Gina
5. Charles	5. Janet
6. Kimberly	6. Eugene
7. Carl	7. Keith

Oakland Raiders:	*Oakland A's:*
1. Michael	1. Jerome
2. Dwight	2. Maria
3. Antonia	3. Michele
4. Edward	4. Warren
5. Ernesto	5. Galen
6. Deborah	6. Roger
7. Matthew	

M. C. Hammer was a rapper from the Bay Area, the 49ers and Raiders both football teams, and the Oakland A's a baseball team. Although we made a few changes by moving children between groups who weren't getting along, these original literature groups remained stable over the course of the school year.

By late October, the literature groups anchored our morning language arts work. And we began to settle into something of a routine—John or I sat at the horseshoe table working with one group as we faced the class, while Belva worked with another group across the room. The two other groups of children worked at the two "independent" centers. John and I liked this new arrangement partly because half the class always worked with an adult, and we had two pairs of adult eyes and ears scanning and listening to the other half of the class. In the mornings, we moved into a pattern of rotating the four groups through four centers at intervals of approximately 30 minutes each. Later in November, John and I became flexible about the timing; we sometimes completed two rotations from 10:30 to 11:30, saving the last two rotations for after lunch from 12:30 to 1:30.

John and I quickly saw positive results from our new afternoon centers and morning literature groups. It both tightened and opened up our teaching. It made it easier to integrate our subject matter, as we moved some math work into the mornings and some language arts into the afternoons.

29 October (John)
    Centers went well. We did three rotations in the A.M. and one in the P.M. Belva did a great job with the math center. She was right on. I had the children write in their journals at one center, and I responded to them during the last ten minutes (of each half-hour rotation) when I had my reading group do some drawing. It was the first time in a long time that I wrote to everyone.
    I think with centers, eventually we'll get rotations so that we can have all four in the morning, and this will allow us to conduct writer's workshop the right way in the afternoon. We could also be creative with the silent reading and listening (books on tape) centers. I know it'll work.

The introduction of afternoon centers and morning literature groups brought needed organizational, social, and academic changes to our shared classroom. The children now had more stable social and work groups for language arts, specific activities to accomplish within a certain time period, opportunities to change activities and tablemates more frequently, and guaranteed close instruction with an adult on a daily basis. The centers and small groups also provided John and me with prescribed time periods in which to teach and complete activities, ensured daily contact with all the children, allowed us to tailor activities and instruction to specific personalities and needs, and extended opportunities to modify procedures and content to increase the children's understanding.

Through both the strength of our evolving personal and professional relationship and our new organizational approach of afternoon math centers and morning literature groups, John and I welcomed our growing sense of structure and order in our classroom. We also relaxed a little with ourselves, easing our obsession with classroom control and allowing ourselves to focus on curriculum and other aspects of our teaching and the children's learning. It was a freeing change.

Yet discipline and control problems didn't disappear. They were still very much with us. And the discipline skirmishes continued to teach us repeated lessons about how the overall quality of human relations in classrooms is of paramount importance in fostering successful and meaningful schooling for both students and teachers. When I got mad at Dwight for not cleaning up, in effect taking out my disappointment and frustration with myself and the class on him, I learned in the moments of his crying, and in my regret, how my anger and his vulnerability resulted from a loss of perspective on teaching to the entire class.

And ironically, it is students like Dwight, in need of extra attention and care, who most need teachers to hang in there with them, not give up, and maintain an emphasis on the positive aspects of their classroom relationships, for these are the students most often looking for trust and structure and predictability in their relations with adults and other children. John and I wished that this kind of insight into our social relationships had been learned in a more uplifting manner, but lessons to be learned (and unlearned) in classrooms sometimes come about through a certain measure of unhappiness and regret.

Bee stings, a hot afternoon, a mother who works nights and sleeps days, a death in the family, a tipped table, a fistful of daisies wrapped in tinfoil, broken crayons, new pencils with full erasers. Creating a classroom with an underlying sense of rhythm can only be engineered by teachers to a certain extent; a programmed, sequenced discipline system can't react to every sudden change. Instead, many facts of classroom life must be reacted to as they appear. And often, as John and I learned, a head-on reaction is not what is needed.

During those long fall months, the participants in our classroom were learning about each other. Lacking a collective history and identity beyond our ascribed roles as "teachers" and "students," it was up to us to create a history. Little by little, like taking bits of cake or a brownie, John and I talked and made changes, working toward what would become a year-long effort to create a stable and yet exciting classroom world for both the children and us. And with every indication of our success, we spurred each other on to make it better.

5

A Sense of Belonging– Diversity and Community-Building

<u>The Trip</u>

Me and my cousin went to the ice cream shoppe. And then we had pizza for dinner.

by Joey

A high level of shared education is essential to a free, democratic society and to the fostering of a common culture, especially in a country that prides itself on pluralism and individual freedom.

A Nation at Risk,
National Commission on Excellence in Education

Had Reading Rainbow *video and popcorn (the class was fascinated with the popcorn machine!) after library on Friday as their prize for moving all the marbles from one jar to another. I congratulated them and told them that I wanted to see if we could get all the marbles into the jar again over the next three weeks.*

Journal, 9 November (Daniel)

John and I shared the personal and professional challenge of fostering a classroom community from a diverse group of teachers, students, and families, not an easy task for most teachers in most situations. John and I learned over the course of our year together, in our efforts to bring a sense of rhythm to our classroom while at the same time fostering harmonious social relations, the value of looking critically at how student and adult diversity plays out in classrooms and schools.

As co-teachers in a shared classroom, John and I learned as much about each other as we did about our students. John and I were aware of our outward differences—Catholic and Jewish, Chicano and white, father of four and single with no children, Spanish/English bilingual and English monolingual, raised in rural New Mexico and raised in the San Francisco Bay area, son of a copper miner and son of a university professor. We were also aware that, based on our upbringing, schooling histories, and previous teaching experiences, we brought varied perspectives on teaching and education into the classroom.

John and I faced, then, a back-and-forth movement between our perspectives of each other, our goals for education and schools, and the daily nuts-and-bolts work of teaching in our shared classroom. These layers of teaching and learning—involving two adults learning about and with each other—surfaced as hidden and yet rewarding challenges. They allowed us to hold our own mini–staff development days over an entire school year.

Our individual perspectives appeared in our initial job interview, when John and I organized the physical layout of the classroom, when we planned our first-grade curriculum, when we met our students and their families on the first day of school, and when we taught and interacted with our students. Even the small ways we responded in the children's journals on the second day of school—John extending the language of their entries while I reacted more to content—revealed our personal approaches to teacher-student interaction and teaching young children to write.

As John and I worked to understand each other and our students, we learned to see the headiness of our position as teachers—to see firsthand the close daily views of how culture and power and social relations can unravel themselves within one small classroom community. In trying to understand what was and wasn't working for us and our students, and in searching for solutions, we had a hard time resisting the temptation to chalk up interactional difficulties to the much-debated influence of "cultural differences" and different "learning styles."

As we limped along during the fall, we talked a lot about why we weren't doing an excellent job of teaching. Central to our discussions was the notion that John and I didn't share the same cultural backgrounds as most of our students. Since the majority of our students were African American, John argued that we needed to learn more about African American culture and history, and find more successful interactional and teaching techniques. But almost in the same breath, John caught himself and recalled that he'd seen classrooms with an ethnic match between students and teachers, and still wasn't impressed with the quality of teaching and learning. Teachers and students of the same ethnicity, then, didn't guarantee good teaching.

At this point in our ongoing discussions, I pointed out the range of factors influencing our difficulties in forging a viable classroom community: we were new to job sharing and to Mayfield, our class had a large gender imbalance, several students were new to Mayfield, and several students needed extra attention and care. John nodded in agreement, but then couldn't help returning to the importance of culture and social relations in teaching. And so our little talks on diversity and community continued over the rest of the year.

Our shared teaching journal served as a place to reflect and share ideas on successful community-building.

2 October (John)
    Let's try using the journal to: 1. Communicate what is going on in the class. Procedures, problems, curriculum, etc. 2. Some theoretical notions on what's going on and why.

4 October (Daniel)

   Just read your idea on theory–am reading Sara Lawrence Lightfoot's *Worlds Apart* and a lot's making sense. There are a lot of tensions in our classroom–between kids, us, us and the kids, us and a new school, and us and parents. Got to go!

11 October (Daniel)

   I read a great article last night about the value of making connections with children, and connections between children and their activities, as opposed to methods and activities themselves. But gaining connections with several of our students is so tough. We can't really be people we aren't, and all we can do is learn from other teachers, the kids, each other, and ourselves. And I guess that's a journey over a long haul! See ya!!

In looking for ways to improve the quality of our student–teacher interaction, develop a sense of order, and feel competent and successful as teachers, John and I became nostalgic for the successes of our old teaching jobs.

   At my private school, relationships with students and their families took time to develop, but from the beginning we had an easier time relating socially. The subtleties of our interactions, the ways we talked and approached each other, hinted at connections in our backgrounds and perceptions of how to be in school. It was familiar "social territory."

   As John and I discussed the familiar, known cultural "matches" from our past teaching positions, we found ourselves attributing our current interactional difficulties to cultural differences.

29 October (John)

   I've the read the article on culture and teaching over and over again. I think that she [the author] has some interesting points that apply to us. The communicative modes of African American versus white middle/upper class children may apply to some of the difficulties we have experienced. I don't consider myself of that class, but am willing to admit that I may have been acculturated to speak in such ways.

John also pointed out that while we both lived in the same city as our students, we didn't live in the immediate neighborhoods of our students. John considered it important to live in children's communities and know their lives outside school. In Arizona, John lived in the same area near school as many of his students. John saw his students outside of school, at the market or park, and knew their situations because he lived it. His students also knew John was part of their community and respected him for it. As a Chicano, John also knew about how many of their families worked—ways of socializing, ways of talking, and how Chicano students and their families may approach teachers and schooling. John didn't have this same knowledge at Mayfield. There was more of a cultural mismatch.

In our first-grade social studies theme, "All About Me," John and I highlighted the special qualities and interests of our students. We followed this theme by studying families and communities. John and I planned activities, books, and discussions to increase the children's awareness and understanding of the diversity of families and communities both in our classroom and around the world. For one activity, we sent home a family tree to be completed by each family. As the children returned the completed trees, I taped them, along with mine and John's, along one wall. Referring to the display and pointing to our big globe, we discussed family origins with the class.

We had a great-grandfather from Cuba; two great-great-grandparents each from Ireland and Sweden; a mother from Barbados; and several generations from small towns in Texas, North Carolina, Arkansas, and Louisiana. African American, Anglo-European, Chilean, part African American and part Anglo-European, part African American and part Caribbean black—these are the labels that can describe and "place" our students in terms of their past and present cultural and ethnic identities.

But as John and I learned, labels alone don't tell the more full and well-rounded stories of our children's interests and histories and talents and agendas. On a daily basis, our six-year-olds taught us that adult attention to culture and ethnicity as critical factors in schooling and school success only goes so far. They are important in making changes for children, their families, and teachers and improving the state of education—yet they don't work alone in schooling. Alongside, underneath, on top of them, there are other forces at work—a sense of order, an ease of social relations, an engaging and enriching curriculum, real and meaningful conversations, friendships, questions. All these and more also pull along a diverse group of adults, children, and their families. And these were the directions in which John and I wanted to lead ourselves and our class.

As with many good teaching ideas, John and I happened upon one by chance. We mentioned to Kathy, a second-grade teacher down the hallway, that transition times between activities were hard for us. Kathy used a "marble trick" that she shared with us.

At home, I ate a lot of toast and finished off two jars of marmalade. I bought a bag of marbles from a toy store, and John and I placed the two jars on the chalkboard ledge by the rug area. We filled one jar with marbles and left the other empty.

With great fanfare, John and I announced to the class that when they did something right (clean up on time, come to the rug and sit quietly, get into line for recess quickly, stay focused on their work), John and I would transfer a marble from one marmalade jar to the other. When all the marbles were moved, we'd celebrate with a class party.

The marble trick worked better than we thought. John and I started by transferring marbles from jar to jar as the children worked. The clinking of the marbles cut across the noise in the classroom, and the children looked at the jar, smiled, and hissed the popular peer "yesssss" accompanied by a clenched fist. Before transition times, John and I specified that we were "looking for people to walk quietly and slowly from their tables to the rug today" or "line up on time after morning recess." We also varied the marble trick to keep it fresh and increase group cooperation by suddenly announcing "two-for-one" marble time, and the chance to transfer two marbles instead of the usual one. (We kept the marmalade lid securely on, as some children surreptitiously made unauthorized marble transfers. We didn't make a big deal out of these transgressions; John and I considered these clandestine efforts further evidence that the children were buying into the marble game.)

One $3.00 bag of swirly glass marbles, two marmalade jars, an easily heard clink-clink across the crowded and noisy classroom, and the offer of a party— in November and on into December, a simple jar of marbles helped build a sense of community by giving us a common, positive goal. The marble idea worked because it emphasized positive behavior and motivated the children to work together in pursuit of a shared treat.

Our transitions improved, fewer children dawdled, and the children exhorted each other to clean up or get into line. When they worked at their tables, Joey said, "Shhh. Daniel's going to move a marble," and Charles, as if impersonating a game show host, announced, "All right, you guys. You guys gotta be quiet. It's marrrrrble time!" With only a few marbles left to transfer, marble fever peaked and the children joined forces to petition us: "We did that right. Can't we get a marble for that?" "We're quiet now, Daniel, can't we get a marble?" "You promised us we'd get a marble if we put everything away."

And it was a lot more fun for us to play Wizard of Oz than guardians of classroom order. John and I relaxed our constant watch for misbehavior, and instead began to see concrete signs of our classroom community finally beginning to coalesce. With a welcome feeling of teamwork and cooperation, we celebrated our first marble milestone with a popcorn and video party. No matter that the popcorn was a little stale (the children loved the whirring of the automatic popper) and that several children had already seen the video (they liked the rerun); we savored the treat and the victory.

The marbles were a lesson in miniature in our year-long challenge of fostering a close, cooperative classroom out of a varied group of children and adults. When John and I first discussed classroom organization in August and September, we wanted our curriculum content, the images in books and samples of student work to be displayed on the walls, and the tenor of our interactions with the children to indicate a sense of mutual respect for our collective cultural, personal, and social diversity. When we began teaching and interacted with our children, John and I tried to hold onto our visions in the face of interactional challenges and a general lack of rhythm. As John and I learned with the marble trick, in community-building, it's sometimes better to chip away at the little places than go for the big picture. John and I certainly didn't want to lose the big backdrop of our classroom's diversity, for it contributed to who we were and who we'd become, but we needed the little changes as we went along. The marbles and the marmalade jars were one small way to build a much-needed sense of community.

More relaxed, more at ease, John and I felt less of a need to scan the classroom as the children worked and mentally prepare for a potential discipline or interactional problem. Like walking along the seashore, we felt as if we had suddenly walked onto a sandier and warmer stretch of beach. And we began to glide a little, move with a little more abandon. This new freedom of movement motivated us to bring in more of our teaching resources and expertise; more of our familiar teaching selves crept into the classroom.

Teaching is rarely thought of as playful and humorous either for adults or children. But our closer classroom community revealed humor that must have been present in our room on the first day, but which we were just starting to see and hear. John and I also started to notice details and little things about individual children. We noticed more of the small gestures making up our daily social and academic life together.

Over a period of weeks, in a game we spontaneously started to play with Nicole, John and I asked Nicole the name of the girl she drew in her journals.

"When are you going to tell us the girl's name?"

"We're still waiting!"

"Is she your sister?"

"I bet her name is Paris."

"I bet her name is Kyeisha."

And each time Nicole shyly smiled, shook her head, and covered up the day's drawing with her forearms.

One day during journal writing, Nicole said, "She doesn't have a name."

"She doesn't?" I said.

When I returned later, Nicole had finished her journal entry and wanted me to respond. Now, a few months after the beginning of school, I began to see the value of John's written response in the children's journals; it was a physical connection with each child's journal, it made for increased contact and interaction with the children, and it served as an adult model and extension of the children's written message and drawing.

"There was this girl," Nicole narrated to me, "and she lived in a house, and she loved to water and watch the flowers grow."

I asked about the girl's name.

Nicole pointed to the illustration.

Looking closely, Nicole had written "Mary" next to the girl.

I smiled. "So her name is Mary!"

Nicole nodded and smiled. This little encounter, a small gesture between us, revealed that for children like Nicole, who are a bit shy but strongly engaged in classroom academics, writing and drawing bring important connections to the social life of a classroom.

Later that morning, I heard a shout from across the classroom. It was Roger. Over by the sink, he held up a sheet and said, "Color, Daniel?"

"Color, Roger! Color!" I shouted back.

Roger, a tall boy with a ready smile and sense of goodwill, had not attended preschool or kindergarten. Though he would leave our classroom in early November to move to another city (and a new student, Jamaal, subsequently joined our classroom), Roger gave the first two months of first grade his maximum effort. Hunkered down over his work, often in a heavy sweater, Roger tried to find a comfortable grasp on the pencil or crayon. Exploring drawing and writing for the first time, Roger had difficulty staying in the lines when he colored shapes and figures in his math, and found working with numerals and letters and words a whole new kind of experience. Although he found much of the work frustrating, Roger persisted with effort and good cheer as he worked alone and when we helped him. (Later in the year, during the times when John and I had just about had it with the class and our teaching, we fondly remembered Roger's shout of "Color?!" and his smile of pleasure in freely moving the crayons across the page.)

The same morning, Jerome rushed over to me.

"Teacher, teacher, I'm going to die. I got stabbed in my lifeline and I'm going to die."

I looked at his outstretched palm.

"I poked myself with my pencil," he said.

"You'll live," I said with a laugh and a wink, "I think."

During one language arts period, the M. C. Hammer literature group and I were reading Leo Lionni's *Alexander and the Wind-Up Mouse*, and I asked the children where they liked to hide.

Amanda: "In my mom's closet."

Kimberly: "I go under the front steps with my kitty."

Charles: "Daniel, not all kids like to hide. I just like going to Big Pizza for a slice with my dad. That's where I like to hang out!"

I asked the group to write and draw in their literature logs about their favorite hiding places. Leaning over his paper, his left arm extended over the table and his head to the side, Arthur formed long strings of randomly placed letters. He wrote several letters without pausing. Unusually for him, Arthur revised the first letter, erasing it and writing a new letter as he sounded it out. As he continued, I was glad to see his concentrated and independent effort, told him so, and we exchanged high fives in celebration; it seemed like a breakthrough moment in his writing and work habits. Arthur read his writing back as, "I like to hide on my bike when I ride around."

Our growing comfort in our own classroom helped us tinker with our teaching. Reading with the M. C. Hammers on multiple levels, I focused on: nuances of the story's language, the children's attraction to the hideout scene, details of their verbal contributions, individual children's letter formation, their use of space in their drawings, the children's sound–symbol correspondences and spelling accuracy, and their overall connections to the task and our little social scene around the horseshoe table. The children's involvement in our classroom activities, and our guiding of the children's learning, slowly grew more fine-grained, more closely tied to the specific activity and the children involved. It felt like good teaching.

Each Friday was our "Reading Conference Day." We conducted these conferences in addition to John's individual and group writing conferences during his writing workshop. As part of our reading program, children checked out books from our classroom library on Monday, practiced reading the books all week at home with their families, and brought the books back to school on Friday for the individual reading conferences. Over the course of the year, John and I had only a certain measure of success with the program. The children became more familiar with a range of books and story genres, learned a variety of word-attack or decoding skills, learned to read and discuss their books with a teacher in class, and experienced book sharing at home with their families. But the book lending proved problematic; it was difficult for all 27 students to remember their books each Friday, for us to find books of appropriate reading levels and interest for each child, and for families to practice reading each week. The books also became lost at before- or after-school day care, or left at a friend's or relative's house or in the car.

The conferences were also time-consuming, even with Belva and Evonne, Steven's mother, helping. With the three of us, we tried to get all 27 conferences completed by lunchtime, but the conferences usually lasted 20 minutes or more and John or I would often resume after lunch when we were alone.

We used a "Reading Conference Sheet" that John devised to chart and record each child's reading progress. The sheet had a space for the conference date, book title, and the child's ongoing knowledge of the book's title, character, setting, main idea, and ending. We used a "C" to denote children's "control" of the basic elements of story comprehension, a "D" for their "developing" ability, and "NE" for "no evidence" of the emerging skill. While John and I disagreed about how age-appropriate some of the charted items were, it was useful to record and see the children's reading experiences over the course of the school year. It also served as a handy form for other adults like Belva and Evonne to use in their reading conferences.

One Friday in the early fall, Maria read a book called *Ruby*. It was the first time Maria remembered to bring back her book, and she was excited. From the moment Maria placed the book on the table, I felt her newly discovered confidence. Maria accurately read some words, and even one particularly long word, and had memorized the entire story. From her skilled "reading" of the book, I knew that Maria and her grandmother had worked on the book all week. At story's end, Maria closed the book and gave me a "and-so-what-do-you-think-of-that!" look. I congratulated her and asked her to read it again. Maria gleefully obliged. On her conference sheet, I noted Maria's exclamation that "Ruby's my favorite character!" and that she "knew the story really well!"

Although she forgot her book the next week (when John asked her what kind of book it was, Maria replied, "A good one for me!"), success with *Ruby* got Maria going in her reading. She brought her books in each week and looked forward to the reading and discussions. Our comments over the next several weeks ranged from "uses pictures and her knowledge of the story" to "Maria was able to tell me what the book was about" to "beginning to decode; knew book fairly well by memory." After *The Pumpkin Patch* and *Fox in Socks* and *The Little Red Hen*, *Ruby* was a distant memory for Maria.

As we began to form a classroom community, new connections with our students came in other, unexpected ways. On the same morning as Maria read with me, Edward whispered to me that he'd an "accident" in his pants. He started to cry. I told him I'd write his mother a note explaining the accident. I gently asked him to calm down, and asked him what he wanted to do. In more embarrassed whispers, Edward said that his brother, who was in another class at Mayfield, had an extra pair of underwear and pants in a bag. At lunchtime, I got the clothing and took Edward to the bathroom. With Edward standing on one foot and supporting himself against me, for there was no place to sit, I took off his shoes and his thick, hard plastic leg braces, and then Edward pulled down his clothing by himself. I helped steady Edward as he leaned on my shoulder, and he put on his new clean clothes. He smiled, and his tight, wiry body seemed to loosen. I then put the plastic braces back on, folded the Velcro straps to tighten the braces, and tied his shoes. The entire changing took over 15 minutes. Edward thanked me and ran outside to recess. I rolled up Edward's underwear and pants and put them in a plastic bag. I went upstairs to write his mother a note. Edward and I had our share of disagreements in the classroom, but after this surprise episode with the clothing, we moved a big step closer. Edward was glad for the quick, confidential change of clothes and I had newfound respect for his courage and determination in facing his daily physical challenges.

Our teacherly efforts at community-building were also helped along by the children themselves. What they valued and prized, such as their heroes and heroines from television and movies, helped strengthen the children's peer worlds, which in turn supported the larger classroom world.

The children's efforts dated back to the beginning of the school year. In September, on his first day in class, Robert drew and wrote about the Teenage Mutant Ninja Turtles in his journal. He drew three figures, two tall ones mostly in orange crayon and another small one in purple. Underneath, he wrote "OlonejtRL Fit." John responded by writing, "Why do the Turtles fight?" This is the earliest evidence of the Turtlemania that magically captured the fantasies and interests of many boys (and some girls) in our classroom over the year.

During free-choice time and in their journals, these boys devoted long stretches of time to drawing and writing about the bandana-clad, muscle-bound Turtles. Galen, adept with a pencil, quickly rose to master status in the classroom for his Turtle drawing ability. Galen was blessed with sophisticated and mature skills as an artist, and his Turtles dramatically leapt, fought, and karate-chopped their way through entry after entry in his journal. Galen carefully outlined each turtle in pencil and added color with crayons. He always got just the right color for the bandanas, weapons, and bodies. He depicted the crime-fighting Ninja turtles with realism: the bandanas had two holes for the eyes, the bodies bulged in all the right places, the numchuck weapons swished through the air like cartoon frames in superfast speed, and the initials of each Turtle's name were neatly imprinted on their belts.

When Galen wrote about his drawings, he gave them a matter-of-fact, caption-like narration: "They're fighting," "The turtles are fighting," "They're saying cowabunga!" "The turtles are fighting the bad guys." As much as John and I, like disapproving parents confronting their children's interest in popular television shows and movies, didn't like the violence associated with the Turtles, we knew they spoke deeply to Galen and the other children. The Turtles and other heroes were modern-day security blankets for six-year-olds.

As an outstanding artist, Galen linked himself with the Turtles, named after the Italian Renaissance painters Donatello, Michelangelo, Leonardo, and Raphael. As the other children witnessed Galen's creations, they copied his style or asked for his help. The Turtles, through Galen's influence, gave this group of children (which included students with the most challenging of behaviors) a common focus for positive social interaction. And they did it in ways that John and I as teachers could *not* foster—their interest in the Turtles, spurred on by Galen, bubbled up from within the children's own peer world. It wouldn't have worked with our impetus. It had to come from the children. And with a sense of allegiance and fascination that adults can rarely sustain, Turtlemania reigned for the rest of the school year. Turtles popped up everywhere. If we asked the children to draw their favorite character in a book, at least one or two Turtles appeared.

Just as Foo Foo captured the children's attention on the first day of school, enticing them to enter our new classroom world, Foo Foo unexpectedly returned to our aid in October.

Late one night, my phone rang at home.

"You're a father!" the voice said.

"What?"

"It's John. Foo Foo had babies. Seven of them," John said.

"What? Foo Foo's a male."

"Well, not anymore. She had seven babies. Joyce and Emily helped me put them in a basket with her so they'd keep warm. One already looks like it's dying, and Joyce said Foo Foo might try to eat or harm some of the others. You'll see them all tomorrow. Congratulations!"

Our students adored the babies. Eager to reverse roles and play parents, they clamored to care for the babies and keep a watchful eye on their well-being. Like something out of *Charlotte's Web*, other students and teachers and parents arrived at our classroom door to see the baby rabbits. Our students put a finger to their lips, cautioning the visitors not to wake the babies. John showed me how to hold the sick baby; I walked around all morning with the baby in my shirt pocket, trying to keep it warm, and the children periodically leaned in to check its status. We all hoped it would live.

At the same time, we started working in our science logs, a variation on the literature logs, and asked the children to write and draw about the new baby rabbits over a period of several days in order to chronicle their growth. Janet drew the seven babies with a line connecting them back to Foo Foo. Ernesto drew Foo Foo leading her litter back into their home. Eugene drew Foo Foo followed by her babies walking in a long line and wrote "iLCTHe-BABeSBueS," which he translated as "I like the baby bunnies." (The sick baby died later that day. I explained to the children that not all babies live to the same age, and that when there is a large litter not all babies survive. I reassured them that the others were doing well.)

But by week's end, two more babies died. The children were really sad, and we talked again about death and living. The other four rabbits grew and grew in the tall chicken-wire cage that a parent built for us. The following week, we let our rabbit family hop around the room during the day. The children loved the animals, and followed our directive not to excite or scare them. The babies grew so quickly that they needed more room. Mona, our farm and garden teacher, already had enough rabbits in the farm, so we decided to raffle them off to the children. We sent permission slips home for parents to sign. John drew the four lucky winners: Eugene, Janet, Nicole, and Carl, who took their rabbits home at the end of the week. (Later in the year, Eugene brought his rabbit back for show-and-tell and a family reunion with Foo Foo. We hardly recognized the rabbit and marveled at its size.)

As our school district and others in California and elsewhere debated the definition and benefits of a multicultural curriculum (our district voted down new kindergarten through grade 4 social studies texts, citing them as "too Eurocentric" and not highlighting the historical and cultural contributions of non-Anglo peoples), John and I learned about diversity first-hand in our classroom.

We learned that there are no shortcuts and no blueprints for forging a classroom community out of a diversity of learners and teachers. Community-building is done over the long haul, begun in the first few moments when children and their families come to the classroom door and ending only when they leave at the close of the school year. It's one of the most critical challenges in teaching to create something from "nothing," to build a sense of community from the first day and then layer and layer it over the year, making it more inviting and more meaningful. Once the foundation is set for a community and classroom participants feel the calm and order, students and teachers can tinker and play with its future.

More relaxed and more confident, John and I saw more of the "small gestures" of our classroom—a shared smile with Maria after her triumphant book conference, a congratulatory exchange with Arthur over his efforts to spell, a playful game with Nicole about the identity of her reappearing journal character. John and I began to see less of our differences and more of our similarities—we were both involved, proactive, searching, and devoted to understanding and improving our classroom. Like cotton candy collecting on a big paper cone, whirling and whirling together in the machine, these little gestures and realizations began sticking together with a welcome sweetness.

Savoring these little advances in building a classroom community, John and I began to let go of the "it's us against them" battle of wills in the classroom. And we slowly started to smudge out the invisible chalk line of control and will between ourselves and the children. We saw how the children's fascination and engagement with the Turtles, for instance, took on mythical proportions, becoming the currency of engagement in their peer world and an important layer of our classroom that *the children* owned and controlled.

Encouraging the Turtle talk and drawings and writings, letting it creep into the children's literature and even science logs, John and I legitimized the Turtles in the "above-ground curriculum." It was our way of meeting the children halfway.

There are no ready-made, pop-up classroom communities. They develop over time as students and teachers get to know themselves and each other—trusting the immediacy of human relations and physical surroundings to make friends, listen to the teacher, write and read, and get into line for recess and lunch. A viable classroom community is complicated—it has to be strong enough to accommodate a sudden call to help Edward and porous enough to let Turtlemania spread from surreptitious desk drawings to journals and literature logs. It was this budding "strong–porous" combination that began to provide the new and welcome feeling that we belonged right in our own classroom.

6

Halloween–
Teaching Today's Children

<u>Teenage Mutant Ninja Turtles</u>

One day there was an old man. He lived in China. His name was
Arokasaki. He taught the Foot clan. But then the master of Kung Fu
came. Then Arokasaki won the battle. Then he went to live in the
sewers.

by Charles

In playing at going back to school one finds again the savor of childhood, delicate and forgotten. . . . What's more, making oneself the gift of an agreeable activity which lacks an immediate purpose is a luxury that costs little and offers much: it is like receiving, free of charge, or almost, a rare and beautiful object.

Primo Levi, *Other People's Trades*

John and I wanted to make room for the world of childhood in our classroom. The Turtles and Foo Foo's babies reminded us that schooling extends beyond specific curriculum goals and the learning of certain concepts and ideas. As John and I learned bit by bit, perceptions of the purposes of teaching and schooling must broaden; they must come closer to the interests and needs of children. Alongside our journals and science logs and social studies units, John and I learned to make a place for our children's interests and their attachments to the modern world of childhood.

Amanda as "Supergirl" in thick red headband and bright red skirt, Janet a witch, Deborah a tiger, Roger a self-styled "scary person" in a long shiny black cape, Gina a princess, Jerome a police officer, Warren as Beetlejuice, Nicole "a girl in a pretty dress," Michael and Arthur as Teenage Mutant Ninja Turtles, Steven as Batman, Ernesto as Donald Duck, and Michele as "a grown-up woman." It was Halloween. Donning masks and painted faces, our class transformed itself into impersonations of icons from a common, contemporary American childhood—from plastic sword-wielding Ninja warriors of the 1990s to older standbys like Donald Duck and Batman.

Some of the costumes had changed since John and I were in first grade 25 years earlier, but our students carried on the same spirit and childhood fascination with fantasy and power and identity. The attraction was all the more meaningful with our students, for they were living with the particular fears and dangers of a more precarious modern American childhood.

Every year, elementary school teachers hope that Halloween falls on the weekend, but more often than not it seems to come during the school week. And it was my day to teach. The night before our parade, I had a mission of my own: to prepare for our post-parade Halloween party. Driving from store to store, I collected the ingredients for what I thought would make for a fun and healthy party: dozens of little boxes of raisins, peanuts, dinosaur cookies, punch, and brown paper lunch bags for the children to color and take home their goodies in.

71

On the morning of our parade, I drove to school with the Halloween treats. It was foggy and cool. No sign of the sun. By late morning, as the pre-parade excitement prevented the children from getting much work done, the sun lifted and spilled into our doorway from the hallway. During lunch, I prepared the classroom. I had talked with Emily, our first-grade colleague, the night before about parade and party preparations, and she reminded me to precut masks for children who came without costumes. It was a good idea, and I cut pieces of stiff oak tag and a dozen strands of different-colored yarn. I also put out the children's journals and special Halloween coloring sheets on the tables; I wanted the children to keep busy while everyone changed into their costumes. (Earlier in the morning, Jerome arrived at school in his costume. I reassured him that he could change later, before the parade; he changed into his street clothes, and periodically went over to his cubby to make sure his costume was still there.)

When I walked onto the playground after lunch, most of the children were already in line, ready to prepare for the parade. Upstairs in the classroom, I sent the children out two by two to change in the bathrooms. A few parents arrived to help. John and I hadn't asked for help; the parents just appeared, but I was glad for the needed assistance. I asked Margaret, Michele's mother, to help the girls change, and I asked Joe, Charles's father, to help the boys. Marta, Ernesto's mother, sat quietly by her son's side. I spoke no Spanish and she spoke no English, and so we smiled and nodded at each other. Some children couldn't wait for the bathroom, and simply undressed in the corner of the classroom. From garbage bags and backpacks and commercially made boxes, the children pulled out their fantasy characters of the day.

As Emily predicted, a few children—Dwight, Kimberly, Keith, Galen, Charles—came without costumes. I called them over and asked if they wanted to make a mask. Charles didn't. Dwight said his mother was coming with his costume. I asked Galen and Kimberly and Keith if they wanted to make masks. They agreed. Kimberly carefully colored and cut out her mask, and I helped with the yarn. Keith and Galen both wanted Turtle masks. Keith tried to draw a mask, but had a certain look in mind and quickly became frustrated and threw down the mask. I helped him draw a Turtle face, and gave it to him to cut. He became more frustrated when he saw children returning from the bathrooms in their costumes. Dwight's gaze continued to fixate on the doorway and the hoped-for appearance of his mother.

Adding to the mounting confusion in the room, Warren tugged at my sleeve and asked about his mother. She had promised to help him complete the rest of his Beetlejuice (from the movie of the same name) costume. Unable to help him, I told him to wait by the door. In a huge, floppy yellow wig and black-and-white-striped jumpsuit, replete with neon pink gloves and inlaid pink collar and black tie, Warren paced the doorway. If I hadn't been so agitated at the moment, I would have laughed at the sight.

Dwight wanted to go downstairs and call his mother from the office. Although I felt bad for him because he didn't have a costume, I said there wasn't time to go to the office. Dwight protested and looked even more forlorn. (If we had a phone in the classroom, either to call the office or to call outside school, I could have called Dwight's mother. But we had neither an intercom nor a phone in our room.)

With an "I'm here!," Laura, Warren's mother arrived. Warren gave her a big hug. Laura, a tall and energetic woman, quickly set up shop at a table and expertly painted Warren's face powder-ghost white, with large black circles around his eyes. As the last child arrived from the bathrooms, almost all the children were up and out of their seats. I wanted them seated, but I was too busy helping children with their paper masks. Then Keith suddenly noticed Galen's Turtle mask and wanted the same thing. But there wasn't enough time for Galen to draw another, so I quickly cut out another one for Keith. Much to my relief, Keith liked it and quickly colored it Turtle green.

As Laura and Margaret took photos of the children, who were getting more and more excited, I noticed another class passing by in the hallway. We were late for the parade. As I announced, "Time for the parade, so let's get into line," we made our way out of the classroom. On the stairs, I bumped into Mrs. Clark, Dwight's mother, clutching a cellophane and cardboard costume box. Mrs. Clark apologized for being late and asked for Dwight. With a shout of "Here I am," Dwight jumped around the corner. He let out a rare big smile at the sight of his mother and the costume box. I said it was fine for Mrs. Clark to help Dwight change upstairs.

Down on the first floor, we joined the other classes surging down the hallway in the collective spirit of Halloween. Outside on the now sunny blacktop, a sizable crowd of parents, friends, neighbors, and older brothers and sisters (who appeared to have taken the afternoon off from their schools) made makeshift visors out of their hands as they looked at the children. I realized then that the parade was quite an event, and my first all-school community gathering since arriving at Mayfield.

The kindergartners, who had already formed a long line as the parade leaders, attracted the largest contingent of media-happy adults toting still and video cameras. I circled our class into second position. Ernesto, experiencing his first Halloween parade in America, held his Donald Duck mask aloft in his hands as he tried to make sense of the scene. Our parents completed last-minute adjustments to their children's costumes, though several children were already falling out of theirs. Laura, camera in one hand, put a few finishing touches on Warren's makeup and adjusted his huge wig, which was making its way back behind his head. Like attendants to a king, two men (one introduced himself as an uncle) flanked Roger and came to his aid as Roger trampled his flowing, heavy vinyl black cape. Finished with final costume adjustments and picture-taking, our still-growing group of parents—Margaret, Joe, Laura, Marta, and Sue, Deborah's mother—joined our line. Dwight then appeared through the double doors, now bedecked as Batman, and sheepishly joined us as Mrs. Clark smiled and waved from the distance.

More classes arrived as the younger children yelled to the older children they knew, and pointed out the wildest and scariest costumes to each other. Many costumes were quite clever. Our first graders stared in disbelief at one third-grader's headless outfit, the fake blood dripping down the front and back of his shirt.

A huge cheer then went up for Jim, who arrived on the playground in his pickup truck. Jim, the school service aide, used to play professional football until he hurt his knee. Standing six-foot-five and a good 300-plus pounds, Jim was an impressive sight on any day, and even more so on Halloween as he stepped out of his truck. In a flowing white cotton robe and long white head-dress held in place with his trademark thick black headband, he was quite a sight. And I wished I wore more than the loud, multicolored hat I had grabbed from home.

Like a giant dragon kicking off Chinese New Year, the parade line lurched forward at the spontaneous behest of its five-year-old leaders, and the entire Mayfield community of students, teachers, parents, friends, and relatives followed. The parade had started. We walked up Walker Street, the school on our right, as more parents and other adults lining the sidewalk waved and smiled. The children waved back, basking in the adulation of their day. One eager father ran back and forth along the street with his video camera, determined to record it all. At the head of our class, I walked backwards and looked back over our class as we walked under the maple trees. Roger's two attendants continued to shadow him, periodically pulling up his cape and adjusting Roger's huge, flopping wizard hat. Halfway down the sidewalk, the hat became too much for Roger; it was making him hot and sweaty, and he could hardly see where he was going. His uncle dutifully carried it for him.

I shouted ahead to Cora, who wore a witch's outfit as she led her first-grade class. I asked for the parade route.

"Up Walker, then right on Cambridge, down Lawton, and we end back on the playground. Not far at all, but the children love it. They love it every year."

And with a twirl of her witch's wand, she exhorted her children on.

At the first street crossing, the kindergartners and first graders delighted in disregarding the stop sign, and leaving two hapless drivers behind a line of 350 pint-size Batmans, Donald Ducks, ghosts and goblins and witches, and football players. On the next block, neighbors on their front lawns and porches waved and greeted us. Continuing to observe parade protocol, the children waved back. Turning right, and passing a tall building, a dozen office workers were seen standing outside and in the windows greeting the children. They seemed to know we were coming. The children acknowledged the applause; halfway through the parade route, they were already famous. The kindergartners then turned right and the procession slowly made its way down Lawton Street.

Back on the playground, our five-block parade completed, parents and relatives and friends took more photos. Sue and Joe said good-bye; they had to go. I thanked them for coming and wished them a good Halloween. Joe joked that he'd try to prevent Charles from bringing any candy to school tomorrow. Laura and Margaret said they'd come up to the classroom and help with our party. Marta came, too.

I thought our classroom party would be a disaster, that children would misbehave given the extra excitement of the day, but it went as smoothly as the parade. The children were only too glad to sit, relax, and cool off. Their costumes were in various stages of disarray, several children wanted to use the bathrooms to change, some wanted to stand and visit other children, and still others stuffed their costumes away for safekeeping, aware that the night's trick-or-treating was only a few hours away. Roger attempted to fold his costume by himself (his handlers had helped him out of his hot, trampled costume halfway through the parade).

I asked the parent helpers to put food on each child's plate. Hot and thirsty, the children first clamored for the burgundy-colored fruit punch. With requests to "just put your cup down on the table," Margaret, Marta, and I poured punch as fast as we could. Laura, meanwhile, began the laborious process of rubbing and washing the Beetlejuice makeup off Warren's face. Making our party a success was a group effort, and it marked the first time John or I had worked with a small group of our parents in the classroom. And I was glad for the unexpected opportunity to share the enjoyable day with them and their children.

As I sat by the sink and poured myself a glass of punch, I surveyed the room. Tilted back on their heads, the children's masks moved up and down as they chomped on the nuts and raisins. Laura finished transforming Beetlejuice back into Warren. Dwight slurped his juice without lifting his cup from the table. Charles told Ernesto about a made-for-TV movie he had seen the night before. Maria and Antonia and Kimberly giggled. Steven and Matthew and Joshua made intricate mazes with the peanuts on the table and talked about blowing up spaceships.

I wondered what Ernesto and Marta thought of it all. Impersonating Donald Duck, Ernesto had just participated in one of the most treasured rituals of an American childhood. Sitting beside Marta, munching chocolate dinosaur-shaped cookies and carefully coloring his paper bag, Ernesto was another six-year-old in our classroom. No matter that Ernesto had only been in the United States for two months. No matter that he spoke little English. (Charles, eager to be his friend, insisted Ernesto could speak "American." He'd grab Ernesto by the shoulders and say, "Que pasa, baby?! Que pasa, baby?!" Ernesto politely gave him a puzzled look.) Ernesto's Donald Duck outfit included him with the other children and some of the trappings of a contemporary American childhood.

The following week, Margaret brought in photographs of the parade. John and I glued the photos to a growing collection we had started near the doorway. As I looked at the pictures, at Warren as Beetlejuice and Amanda as Supergirl, I saw the alter egos and fantasy figures favored by the children. I realized the sense of power and play that comes with traditions like Halloween, and how our parade and party served as an important event for our evolving community.

Mayfield's annual Halloween parade united children and adults in a coming together of our diverse childhoods and adulthoods. In sponsoring the parade, Mayfield as a public institution helped children, teachers, and families feel a little more at home in their school lives.

For our six-year-olds, sadly only too knowledgeable about violence and modern dangers both from television and their own neighborhoods and backyards, school events like Halloween safely frame the boundaries of childhood. It is one way of sanctioning and promoting childhood for childhood's sake. From Gina's princess to Nicole's "girl in a pretty dress" to the waving spectators on the sidewalk, the children relished their made-up day in costumes.

For the teachers and parents, Halloween linked childhoods with childhoods. Much like our community-building efforts in our classroom, the parade served as a common, shared experience for the diversity of teachers, parents, and community members. Given our shared focus on the children, the parade and party helped bring adults together in one of the time-honored traditions of childhood.

One of the joys of teaching and schools is a return to childhood. It can be like a "rare and beautiful object." As I watched our students change into their costumes, I remembered the Halloween parades of my own early school days, the feel of the cardboard and cellophane costume box, and the smell of the stiff plastic costume. Over the years, as our Halloween parade reminded me, the events of childhood serve as fixtures and guiding lanterns for both children and adults to share. They place us in a common time and space, serving as markers both for reaffirming who we are and for establishing ourselves in-the-making.

7

Our Families–A New Parent–Teacher Relationship

My friend is Clarence. He is one year older than me. I am six years old.

by Joshua

Productive collaborations between family and school, therefore, will demand that parents and teachers recognize the critical importance of each other's participation in the life of the child. This mutuality of knowledge, understanding, and empathy comes not only with a recognition of the child as the central purpose for the collaboration but also with a recognition of the need to maintain roles and relationships with children that are comprehensive, dynamic, and differentiated.

Sara Lawrence Lightfoot, *Worlds Apart*

The parent–teacher relationship is an integral part of successful classrooms and schools. But with little in the way of preservice and in-service training on effective ways to work with parents, teachers are left with little know-how for building a second layer of community with parents. As John and I learned during our year together, traditional ways of viewing parent–teacher relations no longer fit the realities of today's varied and diverse family configurations and situations.

And this was a surprise for us. John, working with a more monocultural group of children and adults in the Southwest, knew how to approach and relate to those parents; they shared similar linguistic, cultural, and economic backgrounds. Teaching at my Boston private school, I was familiar with the backgrounds and situations of many of my parents. John and I arrived at Mayfield with a history of good relations with parents, and the unstated plan of relating to our new group of parents in similar ways. As we began teaching, though, and entered into the extended community of our classroom and school, these old ways didn't always work for us, our parents, and our students.

The diversity of our families matched the diversity of our students. In a parallel process, as John and I realized the need to make changes in our class-room organization and discipline, we slowly saw the need to adjust and shift perspectives in working with our families. The learning and the shifts, though, took time and came about through a certain measure of misunderstandings and missed connections with our families. We were challenged to look at our own attitudes regarding the lives of the children's parents, who were *our* peers. It's difficult in any profession to improve relations between adults, and espe-cially complicated in today's urban public schools because of the diversity of adults placed together with the common focus of educating children.

Mayfield's "Back to School Night" in October . . .

Joe, in a new long earring and wild Hawaiian shirt, arrived with his wife, Karen. As they always put us at ease, John and I were glad they arrived early.

"Okay, you guys," Joe said. "Give us the news. How's the little guy doing?"

"Well," John said with a smile, "Charles is doing all right, but he spends a lot of time in class talking about TV and movies."

"That's him," Joe said. "We try to cut down on that stuff, but he just loves it."

Like a mini-reunion of the first day of school, we greeted more families— Annetta, Antonia's mother; Virginia and George (and baby, still in tie-dyed jumpsuit), Joshua's parents; Anne and John (and four-year-old son), Edward's parents; Arthur, Mary, and Mrs. Jenkins, Gina's father, mother, and grandmother. About half of our families attended, and in comparing attendance notes with colleagues later, this was deemed a typical turnout for Back to School Night.

Gathering parents around us on the child-size plastic chairs, John and I stood together in front of the long chalkboard. We disliked the formality of the evening; we felt too much on show in presenting ourselves and our first-grade curriculum and program. Although we were already several weeks into the school year, we knew it was an important opportunity for presenting our classroom in a positive and upbeat light, and for furthering good relations with our parents.

In our 20-minute presentation, we updated our families on the current state of the class ("John and I are pleased with how things are going. We have a nice class, and they are starting to come together as a group"); explained our co-teaching schedule ("We know that we sent you a note regarding how John and I share the teaching load, but we wanted to fill you in with more details . . . "); welcomed families to help in the classroom ("We are interested in help on field trips and with classroom projects. We particularly need help with our Friday individual reading conferences"); gave an overview of our academic expectations and educational philosophies ("Both Dan and I believe in the value of children talking and interacting while they work. So if you walk in or by our classroom and it's a little noisy, well, be assured that your child is getting work done!"); described a "typical" day ("We start with morning meeting. It's an important whole-class time in which we read the morning message, do the calendar activities, count the number of days we've been in school, and . . . "); and explained how we taught writing and how we used it across curricular areas ("There are four stages of writing that young children pass through, though all not at the same time, and you can see examples of the levels in these sample journal entries").

We left time for questions so we'd have a better idea of the kind of classroom our parents wanted for their children, and also to let parents voice their concerns and questions. We wanted parents to hear each other talk, and just as we wanted to build a classroom community with the children, John and I wanted to promote a beginning sense of a common group among our families.

Margaret, Michele's mother, asked about homework.

"Our main homework," John answered, "is to read every night for 30 minutes with your child. Read, read, read. It's very important. For the Friday reading conference which we mentioned, please practice reading your child's book each day. Of course, knowing the book for most of your children right now means memorizing all or part of the book. This is 'reading' for many children at this stage. Not all of your children know how to read or decode the book, but they do need to know the story. Their reading will improve in time. By spring, many first graders really begin to take off in their reading."

Anne, Eugene's mother, asked us to elaborate on our writing program.

"We do a lot of writing," I replied. "John and I believe that children benefit from daily opportunities to write. We write in journals, as we mentioned earlier, and also in literature logs, as well as in science and social studies, too."

Re-creating our tag team from our initial interview at Mayfield, John picked up the cue.

"And we do a lot with what's called the writing process," John added, "We work on brainstorming ideas for writing topics, recording the children's topics on the blackboard or chart paper, and then work in groups to generate our stories and writing. During writing workshop, we use these small booklets made from ditto paper. It has a cover for the children to write their name, story title, and date. The children's stories are kept together with a rubber band in this box. Once a story is written, the children conference with each other and we hold our own conferences with the students. In these conferences, we pay attention to different things depending on where each child is developmentally. After the first draft is edited, we type and publish the story. The child then illustrates the story, shares it with the class, and the published book goes into the class library for everybody to read."

Mary, Gina's mother, raised her hand.

"At home," Mary said, "Gina likes to sit down and write letters to relatives and stories for herself. [Other parents nodded as if their children were doing the same.] She loves to write letters to her aunts and uncles and cousins. I'm so amazed and pleased. I'm very proud of her. I can't hardly read what she says, but she loves writing. She keeps asking me for more paper and more envelopes! But I'm concerned with her spelling. Gina used to spell 'cat' c-a-t. Now she just spells it C-T."

Everybody laughed.

"So what's going on?" Mary asked. "I can't figure it out!"

John explained how we encouraged the children not to worry about correctly spelling every word because it inhibits the expression and flow of their writing. We wanted to promote the children's "invented spelling" and their efforts to write down as many letters as they can for the sounds they hear. Then, over time, we help them move toward learning conventional spellings. Sometimes, as with simple words, we simply point out the correct spelling. We also encourage children to work with each other on their spelling, and brainstorm the letters and combinations that make most sense. This doesn't mean that spelling and punctuation don't count, they do, but that children learn them in the context of their reading and writing.

The questions on homework, learning how to write and read, and spelling are traditional, common concerns of parents. Like generations before them, our families wanted their children to receive a quality education. And what parents often see as quality education is characterized by a focus on teaching specific skill development, primarily in the areas of spelling, reading, and math facts. By asking questions on spelling and on other matters, our families showed themselves as strong and concerned advocates for their children's learning and education.

When Mary, Gina's mother, described Gina's newfound interest in writing as well as her new spelling of "cat," Mary referred to the perennial controversy regarding the most effective way to teach and emphasize spelling. For a number of parents, there's only one way to spell and teachers need to teach it; no sense wasting time with promoting creativity and expression. Although we didn't address the issue at length on Back to School Night, John and I recognized the potential gap and pitfalls between our philosophy of teaching conventional spelling and writing "over time" and some of our parents' concerns with its lasting success and effectiveness.

John and I closed by thanking our families for coming and inviting them to look around the room and talk with us. We ended the formal part of the evening on a warm note.

I noticed Mrs. Jenkins, Gina's grandmother, heading our way. With her purse lodged in her elbow, she looked us up and down.

"Nice to meet you both," she said with a firm handshake. "You know, I attended the public schools in this city when I was a child and so did my daughter. That's three generations of my family. And I'm glad Gina is with you two. I'm glad that the district's tradition of good teaching, especially from such young and dedicated teachers as yourselves, is still carried on."

Convinced her granddaughter was receiving a quality education, Mrs. Jenkins and her entourage left.

The rest of us chatted on until Marian rang the bells to send us all home. Walking down the hallway, John and I felt pleased with our first Back to School Night performance. Our parents seemed satisfied with our teaching and our classroom, and we didn't detect any major signs of parental disgruntlement. John and I had met our stated goals for the evening—we welcomed our families and invited them to volunteer, described our program with enthusiasm and detail, had a fairly good turnout of our families, and allowed time for questions and informal discussion afterward. In terms of the unexpected, John and I felt we handled the questions with confidence and knowledge, and were respectful and supportive of our parents' concerns. We were also glad to see our families listen to each other and begin to get to know each other.

Out in the staff parking lot, John and I joined Cora and Emily, our first-grade colleagues. Lingering for a moment in the still-warm night air, Cora, ever the teller of teacher tales, sensed an impromptu audience and recounted stories of endless Back to School Nights and other assorted gems from her 30-odd years of teaching. In the semi-darkness of the parking lot, listening and laughing with Cora, we were reminded that teaching is really a big ball of rolling stories.

Three weeks later, John and I started parent conferences. As mandated by the district, John and I filled out the "Grades 1–6 Pupil Progress Report," to be completed in October, January, and June. The form asked us to evaluate the children's skills, ranging from "math" to "language arts" to "work habits" to "social development." We brought the October reports to each conference for our parents to read, sign, and take home a carbon copy.

Most conferences went well—John and I communicated our thoughts and observations about the children and exchanged information with parents about ways we could work together with their children. Since the district scheduled only one official conference day all year, John and I only had time for 20-minute conferences and scheduled several families for before or after school or during lunch on other days. Given only one conference day, John and I hoped our conferences would serve as a major bridge toward successful year-long relations with our families. We especially wanted this for the children who weren't doing as well as we wanted in our classroom; before the year slipped by, John and I wanted to work together with the children's parents in order to ensure a successful first-grade experience.

Since John and I had the one conference day and didn't see many of our parents on a regular basis in the classroom and around school, we expected a lot from the conferences. Rather than helping promote good beginnings, though, logistical difficulties in scheduling conferences clouded some of our early parent–teacher relations.

John and I had a string of missed conferences with Mrs. Clark, Dwight's mother. We were frustrated; Dwight needed extra help—academically sharp, especially in math, he had difficulty focusing on his work and getting along with others—and we wanted to sit down with Mrs. Clark early in the year to discuss ways to help Dwight. John and I had both briefly talked and met with Mrs. Clark in the classroom; she delivered Dwight's costume on Halloween, and we spoke on the phone before conferences about Dwight's missing clothing.

Mrs. Clark had sent in a note about the clothing and I called her that evening. Dwight was missing a blue sweater, a blue jacket with a hood, and a green and black jacket. He'd worn the green and black jacket to school the day before but hadn't come home with it. I told her I'd help Dwight look for the jackets in the classroom and on the playground. She thanked me. At this point, I thought the phone conversation was over, but Mrs. Clark continued— she'd noticed Dwight reversed many of his letters and wondered if he was learning to write properly. I assured her that many first graders, especially in the fall, reverse some letters (often "b" and "d" and "p"), but this usually disappears by spring. I added that Dwight might reverse more letters because he was left-handed.

Mrs. Clark then asked how Dwight was doing in school in general. I told her that he was making some progress; he was quite quick and perceptive, but had difficulty following directions, focusing on his work, and getting along with the other children. Mrs. Clark said she was going to get Jerry, her oldest son, to work with Dwight at home. I mentioned to Mrs. Clark that we hadn't received the conference form we sent home, and that we could set up a conference time over the phone. Mrs. Clark agreed and we did. (As suggested in an early staff meeting, John and I had posted a "Conference Sign-Up" sheet on Back to School Night for parents to sign up for a conference time. Since Mrs. Clark and some other parents hadn't attended, John and I sent out slips to these parents informing them of their scheduled conference times. The slip asked them to return it and confirm the time.)

I was pleased with our telephone conversation, and felt that I was making a connection with Mrs. Clark both on a personal level and in regard to Dwight's school progress. Mrs. Clark, though, missed the scheduled conference, and didn't call to cancel. It took two weeks to reschedule. Mrs. Clark missed this second conference, but called beforehand to cancel. Based on these two missed conferences, John and I doubted Mrs. Clark would show for the third conference which we rescheduled for 4:30 on a Friday afternoon. By 3:30 on that day, feeling tired and sensing Mrs. Clark wouldn't come for the conference, I went home. But Mrs. Clark came to school as scheduled. On Monday, Cindy said Mrs. Clark came to the office on Friday, angry that I wasn't around. I called Mrs. Clark that night to apologize. We talked for about ten minutes about Dwight. It was a good talk; I conveyed our concerns and Mrs. Clark offered ideas for helping Dwight. She again mentioned wanting her son Jerry to work with Dwight on reading and check up on him at school. You watch, she said, Dwight will straighten up at school when Jerry comes around.

Dwight's behavior didn't improve dramatically, but at least we were talking with Mrs. Clark. Two weeks later, after school, I was at the Xerox machine in the office when Mrs. Clark walked in. She was there to pick up Dwight, who had somehow managed to miss the bus home. I said hi and walked toward Mrs. Clark. We shook hands across the counter. Mrs. Clark asked about Dwight.

He's doing a little better, I said.

I'd still like Jerry to work with him, Mrs. Clark said, but he's been busy and hasn't had much time. Mrs. Clark motioned for me to come closer. Then, curling her right hand as if holding a glass, Mrs. Clark made a drinking motion, tilting her head back for emphasis. Mrs. Clark said she was trying to stop drinking. A little taken aback at such a personal admission in the office, I said I was glad that she was trying to stop, and I was sure it would help Dwight.

Although both Mrs. Clark and I missed our scheduled conference appointments, we managed to achieve a level of communication regarding Dwight's progress. And it all happened outside the official parent conference. Our interactions and exchange of information came in unexpected ways; I called Mrs. Clark regarding the missing clothing and we talked about Dwight, and when I saw Mrs. Clark in the office, we talked again. And if I hadn't called but had written a note, or had simply said hi from behind the Xerox machine and not moved toward her, Mrs. Clark and I wouldn't have had these conversations. In effect, we met each other halfway, and I learned that good things in parent–teacher relations can come about after missed connections and without teacher planning and orchestration.

Much later in the year, in the spring, John and I finally had a conference with Mrs. Clark. In an ironic connection back to our initial interview for the Mayfield position, when John raised the issue of home visits, John and I suggested we visit Mrs. Clark at home. Mrs. Clark readily agreed. After a five-minute drive in my car, John and I walked the steps to Dwight's apartment. His older brother Jerry, whom we had met at school on a few occasions, opened the door. He warmly welcomed us in. Mrs. Clark came forward and we shook hands. Dwight came around the corner from the kitchen, all smiles and shy that his two teachers were actually in his home. Sitting around the dining room table, we four adults discussed Dwight's progress in school and what we could do to help.

Jerry said he'd work more with Dwight at home and check up on him at school, and Mrs. Clark said she'd read more with Dwight. John and I had brought some extra reading books and a math workbook for Dwight to keep and use at home. Mrs. Clark was appreciative and Dwight, now sitting on the couch near us, smiled again. They gave us an appreciative send-off, and John and I walked back down the stairs and to my car. As we drove away from the street and neighborhood, an unfamiliar area though only a few minutes drive from Mayfield, John and I hoped the home conference would help Dwight. While over the next few months of the school year Dwight did not make as much progress as we expected, the home visit helped narrow the gap of missed connections and misperceptions in this particular family–teacher relationship.

Relations with our families took other unexpected turns. At a faculty meeting in late November, Marian told us that children were hurtling through the hallways at the end of the school day. She'd seen several older children nearly collide with younger children and parents. From now on, Marian said, we were to walk our classes out to the playground at the 2:20 dismissal time. As new teachers, John and I wanted to abide by the new policy.

Two days later, ten minutes before the end-of-school bell, I sensed a growing collection of parents outside the classroom door. It had been a long day, and I didn't want the parents to witness the chaos. Unable to decide between closing the door or raising my voice to quiet the children, I panicked on both options and found myself in the hallway informing Jill, Michael's mother; Mrs. Pollard, Robert's mother; and Robin, Kimberley's mother, about Marian's new dismissal policy.

Robin said okay and left.

Mrs. Pollard, sitting on a chair, stood but didn't move.

Jill, looking rushed and exasperated, said she was double-parked and didn't want to get a ticket.

I repeated the new policy.

Not at all pleased, Jill turned and walked down the stairs.

Later, our colleague Cora told me she heard Jill telling somebody how upset she was with me.

Michael didn't come to school the next day. He returned on Friday, and Jill came up to the classroom just before 2:20. Neither of us raised the dismissal incident. I asked Jill if she wouldn't mind waiting a minute—Michael was our Student of the Week, and I wanted him to take home his body tracing, interview, and collection of letters from the children. I thought that Michael's Student of the Week work, which Michael was so proud of—he clutched the letters to his chest all afternoon—would help mend the fence between Jill and me. It didn't. Jill said not now.

I never spoke with Jill about the incident over the rest of the year, and she never spoke with me. I felt bad about snapping at her, but I didn't know how to address the incident directly. (And Michael never did quite make it to the playground with the rest of us after school; he'd make a U-turn back toward his mother's waiting car.) Later in the school year, I invited Jill to come on a field trip with the class. She came on the trip and I thanked her profusely afterwards. She smiled and said no problem. The fence seemed mended. After that Jill waved and said hi whenever we saw each other. It had taken several months, but our relationship had been salvaged from a bad start—and I gained confidence in seeing that it's all right to be annoyed with a parent and have it all work out in the end.

While John and I were somewhat pleased with the new dismissal policy, since now our parents couldn't wait in the hallway to witness any end-of-the-day chaos, it did mean that we had to gather together 27 antsy six-year-olds, lead them down the long hallway, and bring them outside to their waiting families in a relatively peaceful manner—an effort that was still a challenge for us. The new policy also decreased the opportunities for us to talk informally with our families after school. As John and I learned during our year together, the beginning and the end of the school day are key times for exchanging information or simply chatting and socializing with parents. It makes the parent–teacher relationship more human and immediate. The new directive also inhibited our students from lingering in our classroom after school—for Keith to feed Foo Foo and Charles to tell jokes and Michele to show her journal to her mother. An apparently simple change at the whole-school level, then, had important ramifications for family–teacher relations and home–school connections.

Over the course of our year together, through our conversations and in our shared teaching journal, John and I came to see that some of our innermost perceptions and attitudes about ourselves and other adults influenced the quality of our parent relations. Just as our ideas and attitudes about ethnicity and schooling experiences influenced our interactions with our students, a similar process happened with our families.

Teaching in an urban school in the 1990s, John and I taught children living with single parents, two parents, a parent and a grandparent and great-grandparent, a single grandparent, and large extended families. Several of our students received a good deal of care from older brothers and sisters, and relatives and neighbors also took on key caretaking roles. Some of our parents worked day jobs, others the swing shift, and still others worked nights. A few parents were enrolled in school on a part or full-time basis. As a group, our families varied in age, gender, educational background, employment, ethnicity, religion, and, although we weren't aware of it, possibly sexual orientation.

One morning in October, Laura, Warren's mother, stopped by the classroom to check on Warren's progress. He's doing pretty well, I said—Warren was sharp, engaged, inquisitive, and loved books. From time to time, though, he acted the clown and became disruptive. You just let me know, Laura said, when he gets out of line and I'll drive right over here from work. I said we would. On her way out, I told Laura to have a good day. She said she would; it was her birthday. I asked whether it was a big birthday.

"No," Laura said, "just my twentieth."

I didn't think much of it at first, but later on I thought about her age and my perceptions of younger parents. Laura, a visible and concerned parent who regularly checked in regarding Warren's social and academic progress, disproved the stereotype of young parents not knowing how to advocate for their children's education in schools.

More than John, possibly due to my previous teaching and own upbringing, I noticed differences among the notes parents sent us. Some parents wrote notes on personalized stationary that contained few spelling errors or missing words. Other notes were typed, and I sensed these parents wrote in a tone of knowing what to say and how to say it to us. On our Friday book reading conferences:

> Dear John,
> The book Eugene selected from the [school] library was too difficult for him to read by himself. He did give it a good try, but the subject matter was not as exciting as a Shel Silverstein. He has read other books this week and in particular has enjoyed sounding out the nonsense animals in the book he is bringing to school today. I hope it is not a problem for him to use a home book rather than a library book.
> Thanks for all your help.
> Sincerely,
> Anne Gosse

On a missed school event:

> Dear John and Dan,
> Thanks so much for your notes and updates. Matthew seems so pleased with his class and is proud of what he is doing. I was so looking forward to Back to School Night, but–cruelest of coincidences–October 4th is Back to School Night where our other son goes. Ron will try to get to 201 after an appointment, but if we don't, please know how disappointed we are. So glad you're doing *Math Their Way*–It's great!
> Thanks–
> P.S. Have not seen his library book yet! [*Gorilla Friends*]

On the second report card sent home in March:

> Joshua certainly is ["seems to be" was crossed out and "is" inserted] learning lots about reading, math, and history, and he seems to feel quite positive about school–Thanks for all your good work! Let us know if we can help in any areas.

In form and content, I found these familiar parent–teacher notes.
Other notes were written on scraps of paper and old envelopes, and contained spelling errors and other mechanical difficulties. On scheduling a conference:

Dear John or Daniel

I'm Mrs. Arthur George mom and I'm going to pick him up today after he gets out of after school program will it be alright to have a conference with you then if so then you can reach me at 658-2019 this is my work number, let me know if it's alright to meet with you then. Thank for your kindness and consideration.

Sincerely,

Mrs. George

On the second pupil progress report:

I'm glad she has improved in the class work, and hope she learn not to be so talkative. She continue please let me know about call me at 568-9026.

and:

Edward Johnson will improve his tardy he will do better in his work.

At the same time, I noticed formal salutations in these notes which I didn't see in the others: "Dear John and Dan," "To Whom It May Concern," "Dear Teacher," "Dear Mr. Meier and Mr. Sierra." And the respectful language: "Please call me at your earliest convenience," "Sincerely," and "Thank you for your kindness and consideration." I had never had a parent include "kindness," and found it a warm way to show parental appreciation for our efforts.

The respectful language was coupled with active and enthusiastic assistance and support. After we sent out the second pupil progress report in the middle of March:

Thanks for a stimulating and exciting program. We're happy with her progress. Your efforts really show. If there's something you want us to help her with at home, let us know. Thanks again.

And in response to the second pupil progress report:

Please call me as soon as there is a listening and or a performance problem with him. His report card would look a lot better if I can be informed of what is going on with him in class before it gets too late into the or at the end of the grading quarter. Thanks. I would appreciate it.

And the desire to help over the remaining few months:

> I would like to discuss his progress as of now and what goals or accomplishment I can help him achieve by the end of the school year.

And the ongoing efforts to help if needed:

> I am glad to know that she is doing better in class. If I can be of help don't hesitate to call me.

Seeing notes like these, John and I realized that all our parents were doing what they could, advocating for their children in the ways they knew best.

Jacquelyn, Edward's mother, often stopped by the classroom, pausing with a baby in a stroller (she baby-sat during the day) and asking if Edward was "cutting up" in class. If Edward happened to be in the room, she gave him a little "you-better-behave" look. One day while John taught, Edward disrupted the class and John told him he was going to call his mother. Edward, playing to the crowd and not wanting to lose face, said his mother didn't have a way to get to school. John called. Jacquelyn arrived forty-five minutes later, walking the entire way with the baby in the stroller. When she arrived at the classroom, Edward looked shocked. She informed Edward she'd come any time we called.

Mrs. Moore, Amanda's mother, told us to "keep on" Amanda like her kindergarten teacher did. Mr. Owens, Galen's father, told us he picked two male teachers because he wanted strong disciplinarians. He wanted to be called whenever Galen acted up, and I gave him my home number. Mr. Owens called several times, once calling early in the morning to see if Galen needed a bag lunch for the class field trip. In telling us to watch their children's behavior, these and other parents were fulfilling their end of the parent–teacher agreement as they saw it, making sure their children behaved so John and I could do our job—teach.

Adding to the complexity of our parent–teacher relations, family configurations changed during the school year.

Maria had mentioned her grandmother, but John and I weren't sure if Maria also lived with her parents. Two months after the beginning of school, we found out that Maria lived only with her grandparents. Mrs. Alou, Maria's grandmother, came to the parent conference. John greeted her in Spanish, which Mrs. Alou appreciated, and then the three of us continued in English. In her early fifties, soft-spoken and at ease, she briefly recounted Maria's family history. With just a few details, it became clear that Mrs. Alou was saving her two grandchildren. Maria was in touch with her father, but not her mother, and Mrs. Alou and her husband had taken care of Maria and her sister for the last few years. They were going to court to become legal guardians. Mrs. Alou described their efforts without fanfare or drama; she and her husband were just doing what needed to be done. John and I wished her well and hoped the proceedings worked out. Later in the year, Mrs. Alou informed us that the courts had decided in her favor, and she and her husband had gained legal custody of Maria and her sister.

In our conference with Mrs. Riddick, Jerome's mother, we mentioned our concerns with Jerome's academic progress and his high number of absences. Mrs. Riddick said there were family problems and she was trying to find work. She said she'd do her best to get Jerome back on track. Mrs. Riddick was earnest and friendly, but seemed overwhelmed. During the late fall, John and I continued to be concerned about Jerome's attendance. We tried to contact Mrs. Riddick, but couldn't reach her. One morning at the start of school, Mrs. Riddick came by the classroom. She apologized for not contacting us and wanted to talk with us about Jerome.

I said it wasn't a good time to talk, but we could make an appointment for later in the week. Mrs. Riddick didn't come to the appointment, and John and I never saw her again. Possibly, if I had talked with Mrs. Riddick right then when she came to our classroom, we would have stayed in contact. But at the moment I wanted to get the class organized and start the day, and so I didn't think to have Belva take over while I spoke with Mrs. Riddick in the back of the room. In addition, in the back of my mind, I might have had a formal sit-down conference in mind and so an impromptu meeting at the moment wouldn't suffice.

From November into December and January, Jerome continued to miss more school. John and I tried to reach Mrs. Riddick but the number was disconnected. After winter recess, we calculated that Jerome had missed 33 days. At a staff meeting, Marian asked us to start thinking about students we might want to retain at the same grade level for the upcoming year and send her a list. John and I were thinking of giving Jerome another year in first grade in order to improve his academics.

We sent notes home with Jerome until we received a note back from Jerome's grandmother, who also went by Mrs. Riddick. She'd been ill, Jerome's grandmother wrote, but was feeling better and wanted to come to school to talk. Although the notes had been addressed to Jerome's mother, John and I scheduled a conference with Mrs. Riddick, his grandmother, for the first week of February.

Waiting outside our classroom as John taught our class, I watched Mrs. Riddick slowly emerge from the stairs at the other end of the hallway. A tall woman who had trouble walking, Mrs. Riddick shifted from side to side, her handbag around one elbow, and the other between the strong arm of her teen-age granddaughter.

We shook hands. Mrs. Riddick sighed and took a deep breath. She'd come by taxi, she said, and the pain in her legs was so bad, she needed her grand-daughter's help. I called for John and he left Belva in charge.

Mrs. Riddick sat down and placed her handbag on the table. Her grand-daughter sat quietly at her side, keeping her heavy, silver and black Raiders jacket on. She was the same sister who had accompanied Jerome on the first day of school.

"Jerome talks so fondly about his grandmother," I said to Mrs. Riddick. "Are you the grandmother who's taking him to Jamaica?" (Jerome was fond of saying he wouldn't be at school because his grandmother was taking him to Jamaica.)

Mrs. Riddick laughed. "That's me," she said. "But I don't think Jerome and I are going to Jamaica anytime soon. That's just a little thing between me and Jerome."

On a more serious note, John said that Jerome had missed more than a month of school.

"There have been a lot of problems in the family," Mrs. Riddick said with another sigh. "I'm not going to get into the whole story, but I hope it's all in the past now. I'm now trying to get custody of the children. I'm going to get a lawyer."

We didn't press her for details but John asked, "How long have you been taking care of the kids?" We thought that Mrs. Riddick had just recently be-come involved.

"Oh, ever since they were born," Mrs. Riddick said with a matter-of-fact chuckle.

Several months after the start of school, John and I finally discovered Jerome's primary caretaker. Now that we had this important information, we moved on to discuss Jerome's academic history.

"Jerome's schooling has been a mess," Mrs. Riddick summed it up. "He was in kindergarten at one school and then put in another. His mother kept moving around."

The four of us, granddaughter included, tried to piece together exactly how long and where Jerome had been in school. It appeared that Jerome had attended kindergarten at our school as well as at another school over a total of two years. John and I didn't understand; we assumed that Jerome, like most first graders unless they've been retained or held out of kindergarten, was six years old going on seven.

"Oh no," his grandmother said, "Jerome is seven going on eight. His birthday is in two weeks."

John and I looked at each other. We were embarrassed; we hadn't double-checked Jerome's date of birth.

"Well, there goes that idea," John admitted sheepishly. "We were considering retaining Jerome, but since he's seven already, he's too old and it wouldn't make sense."

We moved on to Jerome's attendance. Mrs. Riddick assured us that Jerome's attendance would improve. I then gave Mrs. Riddick a few books we were reading in the classroom and suggested that any of Jerome's older siblings read with him at home. The granddaughter volunteered. We thanked Mrs. Riddick for coming and offered to call a taxi. She declined and, with her granddaughter at her side, slowly made her way back down the long hallway.

Still more of our child–family–teacher relationships challenged our collective teacher and personal resources.

During morning recess on a warm day in September, Keith walked onto the Mayfield playground from the street. Although it was hot, Keith wore his favorite heavy green corduroy jacket and rubber rain boots, and carried a big red umbrella that he swung back and forth.

"Oh hi, Daniel," he called out with a friendly wave of the umbrella.

Glad to see him, I said hi and then asked why he was so late. Keith said he was staying at his grandmother's house down the street and that he'd woken up late. I asked how often he stayed there. He said sometimes, and that he dressed and cooked all by himself. I offered to hold his umbrella while Keith went to play with the other children.

After the first few weeks of the school year, John and I wanted to talk with Mrs. Burke. Keith missed whole days of school, or sometimes arrived one to two hours late or quite early, before there was adult supervision on the playground. Keith also became easily frustrated with academic tasks, finding it a challenge to concentrate and complete his work. He also was unhappy socially, becoming angry and yelling and pushing other children. John and I wanted to help Keith—for his sake and ours.

He was a tall boy, with a sometimes ready and engaging smile, and we saw glimpses of Keith's soft and happy side. If another child were hurt, Keith often volunteered to help. One day, Robert skinned his knee badly at morning recess. With a tenderness and sense of empathy beguiling their sometimes rocky relationship, Keith cradled Robert's hand and put his arm around his shoulder. All without being asked.

When Keith arrived early or wanted to stay late after school, when there were no other children around and Keith could enjoy more of our undivided attention, we both let our guard down and relaxed. John and I made up odd jobs for Keith in the classroom or let him hold and play with Foo Foo. Keith loved Foo Foo. He loved stroking and petting her. Alone with Foo Foo, we saw a different Keith—gentle, relaxed, fun-loving. Keith carefully picked Foo

Foo up by the scruff of the neck; he told me that he had watched us do it. Keith also liked to clean the sink area and reshelve and straighten the library books. We sometimes talked together as we worked. Working and talking in the quiet and calm of our empty classroom, our conversations were easy and comfortable, far different in tone, manner, and content from most of our interactions during official school hours.

Early on parent conference day in October, Mrs. Burke dropped by the classroom. She said she'd be late for her conference because she was nursing her baby. Mrs. Burke returned later, though an hour late. John and I were eager to talk about Keith and convey our concerns about Keith's social and academic development. We wanted to start the conference and focus on this information, but Mrs. Burke began by talking about Keith. When the baby was born, she said, Keith eagerly helped out by taking care of his new sibling. But the birth of the baby weakened her relationship with Keith. They used to be inseparable, Mrs. Burke said, and had now grown apart.

Sensing an opening, John diplomatically noted that Keith's attendance needed to improve; he was missing school and coming late. We mentioned that Keith said he sometimes walked to school from his grandmother's house and sometimes from his great grandmother's. Mrs. Burke explained that her mother lived at one end of a street near school and that her grandmother lived at the other end. Mrs. Burke's mother and grandmother were not on good terms, though, and Mrs. Burke herself was not close with her grandmother. Keith lived most of the time with his grandmother down the street, Mrs. Burke explained, but Keith also stayed with her in a city a few miles away. With the birth of the new baby several weeks ago, Mrs. Burke decided it would be good for Keith to stay with his grandmother for a while.

We asked how Keith got to school. When Keith stayed with her, Mrs. Burke said, Keith took the subway to school with an older boy. (I had seen Keith's transit card.) John tactfully suggested that it would be good if Keith didn't have to ride the subway to school because he was arriving late, and also wondered if it'd be best for Keith to live in one place. Mrs. Burke nodded. She agreed, but given the present situation, she wanted Keith to continue living with his grandmother down the street and she'd visit Keith as often as she could. In fact, she had spent the previous night with Keith and would do so again that night. Before we closed, I mentioned that we could try getting Keith into a Big Brother program. I told her I worked in a local Big Brother program, and I'd be glad to call the director. Mrs. Burke said that'd be fine; Keith would like it.

Even more than our conferences with Mrs. Alou and Mrs. Riddick, our 20-minute conversation with Mrs. Burke provided us with a poignant and complicated backdrop to our classroom concerns about Keith. Prior to the conference, John and I saw Keith almost solely in relation to his interactional and academic difficulties in our classroom, but after talking with Mrs. Burke we gained a larger picture of the challenges that Keith, as a six-year-old child, faced in his life. John and I took a shared, deep breath, realizing that our efforts to help Keith would not produce quick results.

After the conference, Keith's behavior did not improve markedly. We noted the continuing difficulties in our journal.

6 November (John)
Keith had a horrible day, he complained all day, couldn't get along with anyone, and just ran out of the classroom about 1:00. Marian found him at his grandmother's house. His grandmother came in this morning. She tried to put it all on us—he [Keith] was the peace keeper at his last school and he is so good at home.

John and I finally spoke with Marian, something we realized we should have done earlier, and she suggested a group meeting with Mrs. Burke.

We called Mrs. Burke to arrange the meeting. But Mrs. Burke didn't show for the meeting. We held the meeting anyway and discussed ways we could help Keith. Marian said she'd call Mrs. Burke to arrange another conference. I called Mrs. Burke and told her that I had called two Big Brother programs, but one didn't take children under eight and the other had a long waiting list. I gave Mrs. Burke the telephone number of the second program.

In February, Marian scheduled another meeting, but Mrs. Burke didn't come. By the spring, Mrs. Burke's number was disconnected. Keith said they'd moved. Belva said that while Keith was in her reading group, he said his family had moved to a homeless shelter three cities away. Keith continued to ride the subway to and from school and continued to arrive late. One day, while I was off and John taught the class, I rode the subway home at about 4:00 in the afternoon when Keith suddenly walked into my subway car. Wearing his trademark corduroy jacket, Keith munched a candy bar as he looked for a seat. When we saw each other, Keith smiled broadly. I called out to him and he sat behind me. Like two adult commuters, Keith and I talked about school until I got off. Riding the escalator up, I turned to look down and watch Keith's subway car whir toward the next station. I wondered where Keith had been since the 2:20 school dismissal, and I pictured him munching his candy bar and daydreaming out the subway windows on his way home. I felt both a sadness and sense of admiration for Keith—he faced challenges I had never faced either as a child or an adult. Keith remained in our class for the rest of the school year, and his attendance improved a little, along with his socializing and academics. We never saw Mrs. Burke again.

Since parent conferences are traditionally important meeting places for parents and teachers, they are complicated meetings. As such, they are difficult to script and plan for. Before our October parent conferences, Marian gave us handouts on possible ways to conduct effective parent–teacher conferences. One guide listed possible areas of concern regarding student work and behavior:

1. Weak, slow, and immature work
2. Behavior problems
3. Playground behavior
4. Personality problems
5. Improvement and growth
6. Poor attendance and tardiness
7. The average child
8. The bright child
9. The slow child
10. The new child
11. End-of-school messages

Another described the teacher's role:

- Know the philosophy and objectives of the school
- Realize that the purpose of this conference is exchanging information with the parent regarding the child

offered tips for beginning, developing, and concluding the conference:

- Establish rapport with the parent and begin by putting the parent at ease
- Center the discussion on the child's progress
- Look for opportunities to make suggestions as to how the home may help

and included a list of do's and don'ts:

Do:

- Be tactful, listen closely and sympathetically, try to find out how the parent is thinking and feeling about his child, and help the parent see growth in his child

Don't:

- Argue with the parent, be placed in a position of serving as a marriage counselor, psychiatrist, or chaplain; bring intelligence test scores into the conversation

In our parent conferences, while some of the guidelines helped, John and I needed additional assistance in relating and communicating with our varied group of families. The structure of the conferences, a 20-minute conference during our only official conference day, also hampered a meaningful and relaxed exchange of concerns, questions, and ideas. A different format would have helped—a "get-acquainted" conference with parents earlier in the year, even *before* the official start of school, and then regular, periodic meetings either at school or out in the community over the remainder of the school year would provide more sustained contact with our families.

The conferences did help us learn intimate and personal details about our students, their schooling histories, and their families, without us having to tell or divulge anything about ourselves. Much of what John and I discussed with the families, although some of it was hard to take and sad to hear, taught us more about our children's out-of-school lives and placed their school lives in a broader perspective. The formal conferences also enabled us to exchange important information with the children's primary caretakers regarding such issues as legal guardianship, school attendance, homework, specifics of our students' academic and social progress, and ways we could work together to improve home–school connections.

Since our initial preservice teaching training and ongoing staff development did not address the sensitive nature of parent–teacher relations, John and I were very much learning on the job. And with everything else we had to do, from curriculum development to classroom discipline to learning how to share a classroom, it was a challenge to develop and maintain positive and mutually beneficial relationships with 27 different families. With no formal and sustained training on issues of diversity and relating to a variety of family configurations and situations, John and I made our own way based on our previous teaching experiences and our best intuition. We tried to treat our parents as individuals in their own right, as well as "parents" or "guardians" of the children we "shared" in common.

Upon reflection, this goal of personalizing parent–teacher relations would have been more easily and effectively achieved if John and I had started the year with more resources and information. As new teachers at Mayfield and in the district, John and I didn't know the faculty, the children, their families, or the community. We had no sense of our place in the Mayfield community, and no sense of our role and value in teaching students within that community. As children and their families participate more and more in our public schools and schools become the public institution families know best, teachers and school personnel play increasingly important roles in the education of children and the coming together of adults from diverse backgrounds and perspectives.

Newly arrived at Mayfield, John and I had little sense of our role in this process as played out within the specifics of the school, its families, and the larger communities making up the school. Without our own histories at the institution, parents and other adults had no point of reference for "seeing" our roles in the education of their children. Just starting out, John and I had to nurture our roles and personas as school and community members—both for ourselves and for our parents.

In a simple way, John and I learned that promoting positive and successful relations with families takes time, and it's in the buildup of daily, frequent contact that teachers and families get to know each other, trust each other, and learn to talk and interact in mutually comfortable and valuable ways. John and I attended the first-grade potluck dinner before the first day of school at Mayfield, but not all our families came. If our families had been invited to visit our classroom informally before the first day of school, and if we had provided food and activities for our new parents and children, John and I could have met and socialized with our students and their families, *before* difficulties and issues arose. John and I would have gained an important early contact with our families, getting to know each other socially and learning about their goals and hopes for their children's first-grade experience before the hustle-bustle of the school year.

John and I also could have benefited from talking with our colleagues, and finding out from the kindergarten teachers certain basic information about our students and getting a sense of the children's educational experiences in kindergarten. For our other students new to Mayfield, and we had several, a "new student" form or history could have provided important background information for us, pairing or buddying with a current Mayfield family to exchange ideas and concerns would benefit the new families, and ongoing opportunities for new families to get together with each other and with teachers would help bridge the "newness gap." Without these sources of information and opportunities to socialize and set the tone for our families at the beginning of the year, John and I played a frustrating game of catch-up in our parent–teacher relations.

Working with a varied group of parents, each with their own life experiences and perspectives, which we didn't always find familiar, John and I learned that traditional notions of the parent–teacher relationship need to be reshaped. Teaching in an urban public school in the 1990s, we needed to go beyond our initial teacher training and previous teaching experiences, and learn new ways to reach out and communicate with families.

Back in August, as we prepared for our co-teaching year, John and I gave little thought to parent–teacher relations; we figured we'd continue doing what worked for us in the past. But this didn't entirely work. Faced with twenty-seven different family configurations and situations, John and I had to readjust and muddle our way toward a new set of child–family–teacher relations.

As new teachers, new to Mayfield and to the community, we made our share of mistakes along the way. These missed steps, though, helped us see that productive and mutually satisfying relations between teachers and families are not unlike adult relationships outside of schools. They are prone and susceptible to similar kinds of social and personal perceptions, stereotypes, and attitudes that can lead to misunderstanding and miscommunication in the outside world. John and I also discovered, as in my dispute with Jill over the dismissal policy, that these relations can be mended and salvaged from a poor beginning.

While John and I saw the value of such traditional and time-honored events and rituals as Back to School Night and parent conferences, for they provide useful information and start a line of communication, we also learned the value of *frequent* interactions with families as essential for improving home–school relations. Unfortunately, we didn't see the majority of our families on a daily basis. According to school policy, John and I picked up our class on the playground at 8:45 in the morning, a time when many of our families were already at work or back home. Other parents worked the swing and night shifts, and needed to catch up on their sleep. Several of our children arrived and left school by bus, or arrived at 7:30 in the morning for the breakfast and day care program, and after school they attended extended day care from 2:20 to 5:45 in the evening. Schools need to find new ways to accommodate the modern needs of families in order to promote closer, more frequent home–school contact.

Like other teachers who miss out on daily contact with families, John and I relied on traditional events such as Back to School Night and parent conferences and other parent outreach efforts such as classroom newsletters. As we experienced with Mrs. Clark, Mrs. Burke, and other parents, though, more consistent communication is needed to promote mutually satisfying relationships.

With time and effort and reflection, John and I reached a certain degree of intimacy with our families—we learned their occupations, got to know their other children, greeted them around town, wished them a good weekend on a Friday afternoon, noticed such personal details as a new hairdo—all of which moved us beyond our narrowly ascribed roles as "teachers" and "parents" and closer to "Daniel" and "John" and "Laura" and "Mr. Owens" and "Mrs. Alou." Our interactions became more personal, more grounded in our particular personalities and character.

And this was just what John and I wanted to accomplish with our students. We wanted our teaching and interactions to be personal and connected and specific. Just as we wanted to move away from preconceived notions of a "good teacher" and a "good parent," we wanted to move beyond a "good student." Although it was hard, and we weren't always successful, John and I didn't want to link "good parents" with "good students." It's a dangerous link, leading to the logic that if some parents are not doing their part, then their children won't be prepared for school, and teachers will have to redouble their efforts to teach them successfully.

Much of a teacher's initial and ongoing training is geared toward Everyteacher and Everychild and Everyparent in Everyschool. It's hard to avoid. Yet when teachers enter classrooms, meet students and parents, and plunge into the nitty-gritty of human relationships, complicated and frustrating parent–teacher relations bubble to the surface. And the bubbles do not surface in a constant stream; they appear and disappear without apparent pattern. As John and I learned in building a classroom community, creating and fostering mutually satisfying and meaningful relations with families is a complicated, long-term process.

With just one parent conference, one Back to School Night, one spring Open House, and hit-or-miss weekly or monthly interactions in between, John and I needed sustained, daily contact with our families. Conferences and other traditions should continue, but they're not enough. The scope of family–teacher relations in today's schools really takes in all our perceptions, stereotypes, prejudices, hopes, and dreams of what contribute to a good parent, a good child, a good teacher, a good school. And just like adults in the "real" world, families and teachers relate to each other, need each other, face-to-face, voice-to-voice, desire-to-desire. Possibly, then, when home and school boundaries are pulled away, it can be seen that parents and teachers are more alike than different.

8

New Beginnings–
Teaching and Making Changes

I found a penny. Then I threw it back.

by Janet

1 P.M. There are times when I can't teach and this is one of them. There are troughs in effort as well as peaks and this is one of them. There's a lot of noise, a lot of coloured chalk, a lot of music, a lot of reading, some singing and laughing, but a trough nevertheless it is for me. I'm not of those souls like drifting rain-wraiths out of touch with the essence of life, looking backward through thick tears at some moment departed and weeping that life is not worthwhile. I use those moments.

Sylvia Ashton-Warner, *Teacher*

I felt like I was leading one long, hunching caterpillar. On a sunny and clear December day, I led our class on a walking field trip to see films about Native American life at a local theatre. As we walked along, so did the early morning sun, its shadows staying just ahead of the little movements of the children's feet. At each intersection, I played traffic officer as Belva urged on the stragglers at the rear. Turning to look back over our class, I was glad to see their laughing smiles as they walked and talked. I also relaxed in the freedom of our excursion outside our classroom.

Holding Steven's hand with my right and Michael's with my left, our little threesome fell into easy conversation as we walked. Steven said he was going to Hawaii for winter vacation and that he'd spent a lot of time on the beach. Michael said that he too wanted to go to the beach. I whispered to Steven that not everyone was going away for vacation, and that kids might feel bad if he kept talking about it. Steven nodded. I didn't think Michael had ever been to Hawaii, and I didn't want their different experiences and backgrounds to get in the way of the moment. Yet what I as teacher and adult perceived as a potential problem—economic differences between the two children whose hands I held—wasn't so for Steven and Michael. I perceived a gulf between a white, middle-class child and an African American, working-class child; but as children, Steven and Michael didn't see a Hawaiian vacation this way. Upon reflection, I could have said nothing in response to Steven, or simply said that people have different kinds of vacations, and left it at that.

Our attention then easily wandered to a tree growing in the narrow space between the sidewalk and street. We discussed why some leaves stay on the trees and why some leaves fall to the ground. Michael said leaves change colors and fall to the ground; others stay green and never fall. Again, I stepped in and couldn't help the more teacherly and adult explanation of the changing seasons. We slowed our walk to examine the leaves on the ground, the still-green leaves on the tree, and the colorful leaves about to fall.

Freed from our accustomed and patterned ways of talking and interacting in the classroom, and holding hands, Steven and Michael and I were eager to share an ease of looking and an ease of conversation. It was the kind of feeling John and I wanted to promote inside our classroom. Walking outside, I didn't feel the same almost constant urge to control and direct the children's behavior and actions. As I let myself just be in the immediate ease of our threesome, I almost forgot about the caterpillar trail of 20-odd children behind us—the rest of the class taking care of themselves on our early morning adventure.

I did not plan the walking scene with Michael and Steven; it just happened that they were near me when I placed children in field trip partners. Later, as I wrote about the walk in my journal, I thought about how strongly in-classroom roles and expectations are cemented and how changes in scenery and activity have positive, freeing influences on teacher–student and student–student expectations and interactions.

Halfway through the school year, making changes in the accustomed order of our classroom consisted of both little, spontaneous walks in the sun and larger, planned changes in curriculum and classroom organization. Both kinds of changes became an integral part of our teaching, reminding us that successful and comfortable change needs to fit the evolving life of a particular classroom.

Finding ways to make appropriate changes is a learned art in teaching. As John and I found out, it takes time and often means a careful and sensitive matching of child needs to teacher capabilities and insights *at the moment.* This intricate gauging of our classroom became more complicated as John and I became more closely intertwined with each other and our students—we were both the "problem" and the "solution."

Just as I could only lead the long caterpillar line of children, I couldn't get so far ahead or stand off to the side and observe, John and I couldn't get too far away from our students and our moment-to-moment teaching and interactions. John and I were too mixed in, too enmeshed in the day-to-day dramas and little workings of our classroom community. This made for the challenge of creating change particularly mettlesome; John and I had the most power and the most direct control to change our classroom, but we were also in the thick of things and a more detached and distanced vantage point was hard to come by.

Our teaching partnership, our daily collaboration and teaching journals, helped the process of seeing, creating, and implementing planned changes in our classroom. We were lucky. Our co-teaching position afforded us an ongoing sounding board for looking at how well our teaching was going and how we might improve. Back in early December, John and I sensed that certain changes were in order, but we also knew that modifications don't come easily once a class has taken on a certain character, tenor, and identity. We were also simply tired, emotionally and physically, from the long fall of working on discipline issues and working out the details of our shared classroom. We looked forward to the upcoming two-week winter break as a welcome respite and time away. But John and I knew that a restful vacation would not be enough; we needed to make additional changes in our classroom organization, for instance, modifying activity times so that they would run more smoothly and students would work more independently.

Two weeks before winter vacation, John and I made a few small organizational changes in our classroom. Since our morning centers continued to give us more order, we were feeling more confident to make certain changes.

3 December (John)
   We had the following centers this morning: 1. reading 2. journals 3. ABC (recognizing words beginning with "c") 4. theme (identifying parts of the skeleton for science). All went well. We reread the Thanksgiving stories and pulled out words for the children's "word banks." Writing workshop later in the morning went well. I didn't have any individual conferences because we have just begun.
   In math in the afternoon we had the following centers: 1. tiles 2. beans 3. Unifix cubes 4. inch blocks 5. toothpicks. With centers, writing workshop, and math, there is not much time for anything else like reading the Student of the Week interview etc. But I like it so far.

The very next day, John spontaneously increased the number of math centers to six, and found that the smaller group sizes made for calmer math work.

4 December (John)
   I had Belva do the reading groups this morning. She did great. We only got through three center rotations. The centers were reading, counting groups of four with colored beans, journals, and ABC. Writing workshop is going great. No individual conferences yet. The students are asking great questions, especially Gina and Joey. We should talk more this weekend about it.
   Afternoon math centers were: keys, buttons, geoboards, beans (red and white), pattern blocks, and colored tiles. I think that six center stations are better than five because four in a group are better than five. We also need to figure out how best to have the children *record* their math work.

During the next week, John sensed the need for another change in our morning centers. He was finding that the literature groups needed more time, and suggested that we extend morning centers from 20–25 minutes to 30–35 minutes. I agreed. We both wanted more time for the children to settle into each new activity, and for us to teach the activity and provide a sense of closure before moving on.

I marveled at John's enthusiasm for making these and other organizational changes in our classroom; it seemed to energize his teaching, and it rubbed off on me. Seeing his interest in adding more center activities, and experimenting with the logistics of the process, I felt more comfortable and interested in making future changes.

In looking at how John and I altered our classroom in mid-year, I noticed a key difference in what powered our teaching: while I enjoyed making changes at the curricular and interpersonal levels in the classroom, John loved reversing a trend in classroom organization and training the children to participate in a new structure or routine. John loved the action of setting new center activities and procedures in motion. Standing in the middle of the room like an army sergeant at roll call, John explained each new activity and instructed the children on how to rotate through the centers.

Seeing John's excitement about making changes in our centers, I realized that teachers don't need to make the *same* kinds of changes and in the same ways. In addition, remembering my feelings of doubt about working with John earlier in the school year, I now saw more clearly that some of our differences—as seen in the varied way we approached and implemented classroom changes—proved to be a strength to our teaching partnership and the overall effectiveness of our shared classroom.

Like a new spark plug, even small organizational changes rejuvenated John. I sensed it in his teaching and saw it in his journal comments. The changes enlivened and brightened the daily pattern of teaching and interaction in our classroom, and served as a reminder that teachers need to make changes as much for themselves as for their students, and that teachers have considerable power and control over the direction of their classroom worlds.

As one successful change led to another, after winter vacation John and I returned with renewed energy to improve our shared classroom over the second half of the year.

7 & 8 January (John)

Centers have been going great. In reading, I think we need to model all of the options for literature projects: plays, puppets, mobiles, posters etc., for the students before we give them a choice in the centers. I did the play of "The Three Billy Goats Gruff" with all of the groups. Maybe you could run through another project with them, with either this story or another. I also would like to run through all the classics with the class, sort of a "story immersion." You know, maybe we could do "The Three Little Pigs," "Jack and the Beanstalk," "Little Red Riding Hood," and "Cinderella."

Mayfield's book room had a good selection of boxed, multiple-copy selections from children's literature, but only a handful of our students could read them. We read the easiest-to-read of these books in our literature groups, reading the story together, and pointing out the predictable language patterns to aid the children's memorization of the text. Loving the plot of the stories and the drama opportunities, the children easily memorized "The Three Billy Goats Gruff." We had unexpectedly hit on a winner. The children delighted in taking turns acting the parts. John thought Joey a born actor, a natural Troll—"He has the perfect voice. He gets down in a crouch and delivers his lines perfectly. He was so good that I kept him as the Troll as the kids switched parts."

"The Great Big Enormous Turnip" is a classic tale about an old man who plants a turnip and implores it "to grow strong" until it becomes "big and enormous." In the version in our published basal reading series, the old man "went to pull it up, he pulled and pulled again, but he could not pull it up." So "he called the old woman," and the "old woman pulled the old man" who in turn pulled the turnip. The illustrations show the old man leaning back and pulling the top of the great big enormous turnip and the old woman, also leaning back at an even more severe angle, pulling the old man by his suspenders. The old man continues to call more helpers—the old woman's granddaughter, a black dog, a cat, a mouse—until they finally pull up the turnip. The children enjoyed the illustrations, the fantastic hugeness of the turnip, the happy ending, and most of all the slapstick comedy of the characters all falling down in a heap at the end.

After reading the story at the horseshoe table, we moved a few steps over to the library for the dramatic reenactment. I took the big globe from the windowsill and pretended it was the turnip. With the "great big enormous turnip" on the library rug, we dramatized the story, taking turns as the characters. Surprisingly, the boys didn't mind playing the "girl" characters and the girls the "boy" characters, and all the children loved impersonating the animals. Tall Deborah was a perfect old man, and she did her best to make herself as small as the mouse. The shorter Eugene stretched himself out as tall as possible for his old man role and had no difficulty curling up as the mouse. Caught up in the pretend of their roles, the children became more and more animated and dramatic until Amanda finally got carried away and rolled on the turnip, cracking the globe. Although I was annoyed with her, I had a hard time getting mad; I was so pleased with their engagement and cooperation.

The class also loved reading "The Little Red Hen." They took to chanting the repetitive phrases and were in solidarity with the hen for having to plant, water, harvest, process, and cook the wheat without any help from her supposed friends. In order to get the children thinking about the characters in the stories, I created a simple worksheet with six boxes. In the 49ers literature group, the children drew pictures of the little red hen and her three "friends." Only Steven noticed that two empty character boxes remained, and solved the problem by creating two entirely new characters.

John also advocated changes to our writing program, which already consisted of writing workshop taught by John a few times a week, as well as journals and other writing activities connected to our story time and theme work.

> *7 & 8 January (John)*
> With Belva, I had the students do storytelling and recording. First day tell a story and then draw/write about your favorite part. Second day write the beginning, middle, and end. Third day, tell again and finish beginning, middle, and end. Fourth day expand the story into a book. In this way, writing workshop is kind of modeled in a small group.

While I agreed with John that we needed more well-thought writing activities to enrich language arts in the centers, I found his plans too rigid and the beginning-middle-end structure too abstract for first graders. We agreed to disagree and John worked on story structure while I emphasized more open-ended writing connected to art activities.

Implementing these curricular and organizational changes, John and I found ourselves more closely focusing on the details of our teaching and the children's social and academic involvement. On the Friday morning of our first week back from vacation, I had my center groups do two worksheets on quilts. The first came from an issue of *Scholastic News* that appeared in my mailbox. I explained the sheet to the children: they had to examine the five quilt designs and decide which ones corresponded with the given names of "moon over the mountain," "fan," "windmill," and "bear's paw." A space at the bottom allowed the children to make their own designs. Surprisingly, Amanda, an accomplished reader, and Eugene, a less experienced reader, both finished the sheet at the same time. All the children did well on the sheet.

The second paper involved creating a quilt design. The children had to color four different shapes on the quilt by coloring the triangles green, squares blue, diamonds orange, and rectangles black. A good example of a traditional worksheet, it is designed to introduce, teach and reinforce such basic skills as identification of geometric shapes and sorting shapes into categories. The children then had to count and record the total number of each shape and write the numeral on a line beside that shape. Again, most of the children did well. Robert, though, found the task challenging. I tried a few different ways to explain the task, but none helped, and so I encouraged him to color the shapes as he wished. Although Joey noticed that "Robert's not doing it right," his tone didn't have an edge to it and Robert didn't take offense. Robert was pleased with his efforts as he slid the crayon across the shapes.

At various times during the year, John and I debated the educational value of worksheets. John favored creative and developmentally appropriate tasks and activities tailored to children's individual levels of interest and experience. And so did I. But in my previous private school teaching, I had placed children in "ability groups" to read leveled readers with accompanying workbooks and worksheets, the classic structure of low, middle, and high reading groups deeply embedded from my own school days and my teacher training. Over time, I saw that this academic and social organization, though, placed constraints on mobility between groups and influenced children's sense of competence as emerging readers, writers, and social members of a classroom community.

In our shared classroom at Mayfield, when I gave out the two quilt sheets and saw how the work gave our students a set structure within which to work and a quick, concrete sense of accomplishment, I reconsidered the value of worksheets. And so here and there, primarily in math and language arts, I used the occasional worksheet. Depending on the sheet and the particular child, feelings of success may or may not have been tied to new levels of conceptual understanding; sometimes the children's good feelings came from the act and evidence of completing a set, prescribed task. Further, since a worksheet gave all the children the exact same task in our heterogeneous, mixed-ability groups, the children had a *common* focus for working and helping each other—for example, there was only one color for the triangles and only one correct answer for the total number of triangles in the quilt design.

The sheets also gave certain children with less advanced academic skills something more "to go on." They did not face a blank page and the possible sinking feeling of not drawing or writing well. Yet certain caveats arose with the worksheets. I had to guard against the frequent problem that the very procedure of the sheet, like writing in the numerals from 10 to 1 in boxes to represent a rocket's countdown, was *more* complicated and challenging than the intended concepts to be learned, such as counting and adding on by one. Some children, though, used this to their advantage; when Eugene finished his quilt sheet with Amanda, I realized that Eugene had made up for the reading differential by quickly getting the trick of the sheet's procedure. He side-stepped the content by focusing on the graphic procedure of the page. This kind of insight, though, can be deceiving because when children successfully "do" the sheet, they may not actually understand or internalize what they did. What is "learned," then, can become fuzzy and hard to see.

Not only did some of our classroom modifications lead to others, they strengthened our teaching partnership. John and I felt stronger as a teaching team, and we began to have more fun. The children's engagement with the stories and Joey's Troll rendition and Deborah's mouse role were some of the mini-highlights of our year together, and defined those moments when our teacherly changes brought on a more comfortable and easygoing sense of engagement with the content of our curriculum and the spirit of our social interactions. And although late arriving, it was the kind of dual "teaching-learning" we had wanted from the beginning of the year.

Other welcome changes came from outside our classroom. Since Amanda read well and was bored in our reading groups, I thought of having her read in a second-grade classroom. I approached our second-grade colleague, Kathy, and explained Amanda's situation. She agreed to have Amanda join one of her reading groups. I called Mrs. Moore, Amanda's mother, who said that whatever we thought best for Amanda was fine with her. At first, Amanda was reluctant to go ("it's too hard down there," she'd say, and she missed her classmates) but after a week Amanda went readily. I checked in with Kathy, who said that Amanda was reading right along with the others and that her behavior was perfect. John and I were happy for Amanda, and pleased that our reaching out to a colleague had worked so well.

Just before winter vacation, Geoffrey, the music teacher hired by the PTA in late November (paid by PTA fundraising monies), staged a winter holiday songfest with only a few weeks' rehearsal time. On the Thursday night before our winter vacation, over a dozen of our students returned to Mayfield with their families to sing at the nighttime concert. The children dressed in their Sunday best, the girls in black shiny shoes and dresses and the boys with their shirts tucked in.

Cora, Emily, and I ushered our first graders onto the risers on the stage, stood in the wings, and like proud parents stood ready to mouth the words to the "Banana" song and exhort our children to sing loud and well. Several of our students proudly held signs indicating various ethnic and national groups.

Nicole—Native Alaskans
Eugene—Native Americans
Gina—Russians
Janet—Incas
Maria—Mayans

Ernesto—Chileans (he loved representing his native country)
Joshua—Mexicans
Edward—Canadians

After the kindergartners performed, Geoffrey announced over the PA system that "the first grade would like to do the banana song for you. This is a song about people all over the world and throughout history who have liked bananas." The crowd laughed. Geoffrey cued the 50 or so very nervous first graders. As each group was mentioned, "Mayans like bananas," up went Maria's sign. "Russians like bananas," up went Gina's "Russian" sign. Next, the children sang a festival song from Nicaragua's North Atlantic Coast and "Christmas Time's a Comin'" by Tex Logan. With a roar of approval and several rounds of flashing cameras, we helped our students off the stage. As we led the children back to the classrooms, we told them how proud we were of their singing. I smiled inwardly at how mature our class looked and acted, and I liked the mix of children, songs, parents, and the general community feeling of the evening. It felt like Mayfield's Halloween parade.

In the middle of January, through more PTA fundraising and district monies, Marian hired part-time art and physical education teachers. The staff was pleased. Our class would receive art for one hour over five weeks and PE for half an hour for twelve weeks. Although the art teacher had a hard time teaching our class and John and I stepped in to get the children's attention and restore order, the children liked the art projects and we had the opportunity to observe our class from a distance. The PE teacher was excellent. Organized, enthusiastic, and creative, she provided a stimulating and rewarding 30 minutes of exercise and games. She was an excellent model for both girls and boys.

At the same time, Roger, the school psychologist who only worked at Mayfield on a part-time basis, started a small-scale program for students in need of self-esteem and confidence building. John and I filled out a questionnaire regarding the academic and social progress of several of our children, and Roger compiled a list of the neediest children for the program based on the results. Since Roger had a limited number of people helping him, we could only select one child for the program. We selected Dwight; his interactions with others had not improved dramatically and he could benefit from the extra positive attention and care. When I called Mrs. Clark, though, she declined the offer. John and I then selected Steven, and Bob and Evonne, his parents, signed the consent form. Steven remained in the program for the remainder of the school year, and his parents were pleased that he worked cooperatively and successfully on the program's tasks and games.

These and other out-of-class changes helped the children and John and me feel more connected to the school in general. We felt part of something larger. The changes also enriched our still-evolving classroom community, affording new opportunities for our children to participate and learn in the still-new world of school.

Our single most important change came in late January. John and I decided to change our teaching schedule and split the curricular responsibilities. The decision happened more by circumstance than design; John's second-semester classes were in the mornings and so we couldn't keep our whole-day rotation. John suggested a morning/afternoon split from Monday through Thursday and a continued alternating of Fridays. I agreed. I wanted more contact and communication both with the children and the two of us, and a morning/afternoon would split would give us that opportunity. I agreed to teach the mornings and John agreed to the afternoons.

We also decided to divide the curriculum. John would teach math and science and writing workshop, which he loved, and I would teach the rest of language arts and social studies. John and I both liked the new schedule and curriculum sharing; it felt more streamlined and we looked forward to more contact with the children and each other. We also felt a sense of relief. The new system felt more manageable and more contained. We were both "jazzed," and eager to implement the new changes.

But over the weekend, John's wife called me at home. John was sick, she said, in the hospital suffering from some as yet undiagnosed ailment. He'd love to see me. I drove to the hospital that afternoon. High up on the 10th floor, John lay curled in a fetal position as the bright afternoon sunlight emptied into the empty hospital room. John looked pale and weak. He didn't move as I entered. I was shaken to see him like this, lying immobilized and weak. I handed John a bag of chocolate croissants, his favorites. John thanked me. He complained of a horrible splitting headache and fever, and showed me his elbow, which had ballooned to the size of a baseball. The doctors weren't sure of the problem; John thought the elbow was possibly infected by a spider bite. John said that he'd never been so sick. I told him not to worry, that I'd take care of things in the classroom.

I called for a substitute teacher to take John's days, wrote the lesson plans, and taught when I couldn't get a substitute. The children missed John. I told them John was sick and would probably be back next week. I visited John again in the hospital, and he was sitting up in bed. The swelling in his elbow had not gone down, but he looked better. I gave him the get-well cards from the children, and John opened each one, slowly commenting on each child's drawings and writing. The doctors had still not determined the cause of the infection and were debating lancing the elbow to drain the fluid. They finally did toward the end of the week, and John was released on Saturday.

John returned to the classroom just before lunch on Monday. I didn't bother stopping the children from running to give John a big whole-class hug. John bent down and hugged back as many children as he could. I was glad to have John back. I felt like the other half of my teaching self had returned. John felt much better. He had a small patch over his elbow, the swelling was gone, and he thought he had infected the elbow from scratching it. But John still kept alive the story of a spider bite—and in the spirit of Joey's tall tales, told the children gathered around him on the rug after lunch about the big spider at his home.

Our new schedule change didn't entirely make our teaching "a piece of cake," as Charles was fond of saying, but John and I cautiously enjoyed our newfound sense of rhythm and sense of competence. Responsible now for two curriculum areas each, John and I concentrated on more crisp planning, better-integrated activities, and closer follow-up and assessment. Teaching and working with the children on a daily basis, we had more consistent and stable contact with the children. If John and I had started the school year with our new morning/afternoon schedule, we might well have avoided a number of our discipline problems and general lack of classroom order. The children sensed and welcomed the new schedule, and looked forward to the daily sighting of John and Daniel together at the lunchtime break; all of us were strengthened by the renewed sense of teamwork and community.

Our newly instituted daily check-in time promoted closer professional and personal ties between John and me. Six months after we started teaching together, we got to know each other better. John often came in early before I dismissed the children for lunch, catching the end of my morning teaching which allowed him an early sense of the mood of the class. His presence also gave the children a sighting of John and advance notice of the imminent changing of the guard, and helped prepare the class for our midday switch.

John and I often ate lunch together in the classroom. John would bring in an extra chocolate croissant or sandwich, and we sat on the small chairs talking about our students, our personal lives, current events, the state of education, and other topics both personal and professional. Our lunchtime chats reminded me that professional partnerships between adults in education and teaching are as much built on the personal and social as on traditional areas of professional concern.

With the changes in our classroom came a new and welcome sense of ease and comfort with both ourselves and with our students.

. . . At morning meeting, I wrote a riddle on the chalkboard: "I am a number between 67 and 69. Who am I?"

Gina raised her hand.

"An old man," she said.

I smiled at that one.

. . . I put up another riddle: "What did the dog say when it sat on the sandpaper?"

Matthew raised his hand.

"Daniel, 'sandpaper' is a compound word."

We then brainstormed other compound words.

Amanda suggested "Chicken Little" and Deborah "Oakland."

. . . During music, when we were singing a spiritual, Joey leaned over to me and said confidentially, "God's wife is Mother Nature."

. . . While I was a running an activity at the horseshoe table, Matthew came over and informed me in his typical matter-of-fact manner, "Ernesto just said 'shit.'" I did my best not to burst out laughing.

. . . During a discussion on Martin Luther King, Jr., Amanda said that "Harriet Tubman helped Martin Luther King to freedom."

Several months after starting the school year, I finally found myself laughing and losing myself in the moments of teaching and interacting. At first the children were surprised at my laughter; it was such a new sight and sound in our room. It felt good to let myself go a bit, and I didn't panic about losing control of the class and descending into chaos.

When I taught at my old private school, I taught first by personality and second by method. When John and I made changes in our classroom and other welcome changes happened at the school level, I found that my personality slowly came back into my teaching. I laughed with Joey that "God's wife is Mother Nature," and I slowly experienced more of the ease of conversation and interaction that characterized my walk in the sun with Michael and Steven. It was a long-overdue feeling, and one that nourished our little interactions and the overall feeling of community. And in looking back on the value of making changes in our teaching and classroom, John and I learned that change in the classroom does not so much tighten as loosen things, freeing teachers and students to be less like they should be and more like they want to be.

9

Robert–
Lessons from a Child

This is my friend and me.

by Joey

I like to go to school and play by myself. Play soccer by myself outside and play on the tire swing. And play by myself and go somewhere where it's quiet. And go to Irene's room and do work and come upstairs and sit down and do work.

Robert, Class video, June

"Do." "Play." "Go." "Work." A tall, thin boy with a quick walk and ready smile, Robert used simple and yet powerful verbs to articulate his strong desire to be connected to the social and academic worlds in our classroom and school. Over the course of the year, John and I worked to give Robert a successful and enjoyable first-grade experience. In our efforts, which brought us beyond our interactions and teaching of Robert in our classroom, John and I learned a great deal about the intricacies of helping just one child.

Early in September, John and I noticed Robert's difficulty with certain social situations and academic tasks. Mindful that several children, including Robert, needed extra assistance, John and I looked at our available resources. At the time, we were told that Belva, who was paid with Mayfield's share of federal Chapter I funds, was supposed to work with underachieving students based on a district kindergarten assessment measure. Although Robert was new to Mayfield and our office didn't yet have a "cumulative" file for him, we placed Robert with a small group of students working with Belva for an hour a day of extra attention.

In addition, we assigned two undergraduate students (who received credit for their tutoring from their university) to work with Robert and Roger two mornings a week. John and I kept an extra eye on Robert, doing what we could to help him make friends and successfully participate in our academic activities. We orchestrated all our resources and extra "hands" to help Robert, but given our large and energetic class, John and I knew that we needed additional assistance.

In late September, John and I were walking by the school office when Erika, the speech and language teacher (who only worked at Mayfield two afternoons a week due to budget cuts), stopped us in the hallway. She wanted to know if Robert was in our class. We said yes. Erika said that Robert had been in a "special day class," an all-day class for children considered to have serious disabilities, when he was in the district two years earlier. John and I weren't aware of this history.

When we initially met Mrs. Pollard, Robert's mother, on Robert's first day in our classroom, she said Robert had attended a private school the previous year for first grade, and that although Robert had done well and improved, she thought another year of first grade would be the best placement. John and I, not knowing Robert, didn't think too much of her request and said fine.

When we had worked with Robert for a few weeks in our classroom, and heard from Erika about Robert's earlier placement in the district, John and I started to wonder about the best placement for Robert. What followed from September to June is a chronicle of our efforts to provide extra services and the best educational environment for Robert. It proved quite difficult at times, an extra challenge for John and me beyond the already taxing necessity of molding our class into a successful learning community. In our efforts to help Robert, various subplots unfolded with their own "lessons learned"—about teachers' views of their own competency and success, about teachers as advocates for themselves and their students, the complicated professional labyrinth that often arises when "regular education" meets "special education," and the sensitive and intimate nature of working with families of students in need of extra assistance.

As September turned into October, John and I felt that Robert's difficulties were beyond our expertise and resources. We needed outside help. At this point, like many classroom teachers, we sought outside assistance in the form of special education. John and I weren't sure whether we wanted extra services for Robert in our classroom, a "pull-out" program for part of the school day, or an entirely new placement in a special day class either at Mayfield or at another site. At the time, John and I had little idea of the professional gulf that can exist between "regular" and "special" education. These two camps can be characterized by differences in educational jargon, testing measures, access to student files, district and state rules and regulations, paperwork and forms, parental consent guidelines, administration approval and contact, and general educational philosophies.

As new teachers inexperienced with the maze of politics and procedures in gaining special education services, John and I learned as we went. I had taken a mainstreaming class as a student teacher, but the class didn't address specific ins and outs of procuring services for students in need. When I taught at my Boston private school, children in need of extra academic assistance worked with a reading teacher or families paid extra money for the private tutors housed at the school. John had some experience with special education teaching in the Southwest, but he was more familiar with bilingual education laws and regulations. As teachers with little or no experience advocating for additional student services, John and I were in an uncharted area of the educational "system" as we tried to help Robert. And it was often a dizzying and frustrating effort.

As we started the paperwork in motion for extra services, John and I continued to do what we could to help Robert in the classroom. We knew we could be more sensitive to Robert's social and academic needs, helping him make friends and find ways to get along with peers, and structure activities and modify our directions to be more manageable and flexible for him.

Our early efforts to assist Robert were partially undermined by the general lack of stability and predictability characterizing our classroom. Like many students in need of extra attention and care, a calm and orderly learning environment would have had a calming effect on Robert by decreasing distractions and ensuring stability. When other children got off task as they worked, Robert didn't want to be left out and imitated their actions. But this often rattled other children, and Robert had a hard time getting back to his work.

As six-year-olds, our first graders were developmentally able to distinguish differences between each other in increasingly fine nuances of language, action, thought, and feeling. While John and I tried to use this developing sensitivity to promote feelings of group solidarity and group problem-solving, it also meant that the children noticed differences and similarities among each other. Several children were particularly bothered by some of Robert's behavior, and through the fall months, there was a slowly growing perception within the underground peer world that Robert was somehow set apart from the other children. And this led to skirmishes and disputes between Robert and certain peers.

Playing Monday morning quarterback, a quick reversal of this dynamic on our part might have turned the children's attention from Robert's social and academic difficulties to something more positive and kept Robert more included in the peer fold. Early in the school year, we might have gathered the children on the rug for a whole-class discussion and said: "We know that some of you complain about Robert doing this and doing that. But he's not the only one doing it. What's really important here is that we come together and discuss why it's important for *nobody* to throw things and call names and bother each other. Remember when we made our class rules on the first day of school? What does it say here on our list? Why are these rules still important?" Regular class discussions about *general* underlying issues of respect, cooperation, and conflict resolution might have shifted the focus from Robert to our entire classroom community. At the time, though, John and I hadn't instituted a whole-class meeting routine, and we weren't any more able to provide a stable mini-world for Robert than we could for the rest of the children.

Later in the year, a fellow graduate student conducted a research project in our classroom and happened to focus on Robert. Based on this research project, the study concluded that the kind of child-centered learning involving lots of peer talk and interaction as found in our classroom excluded children like Robert. Left to rely on their own resources by teachers not running structured and teacher-directed classrooms, children like Robert may not have the social and academic wherewithal to succeed. The researcher concluded that in classrooms with our kind of social and academic organization, some children remain on the social and academic periphery and suffer negative interactions with peers.

When John and I read the study and the researcher's conclusions based on our classroom, we first felt a sense of guilt that we had done wrong by Robert. But as we talked about it, we reminded ourselves of our initial and ongoing commitment to a classroom community based on the educational value of student choice and control, talk, and social interaction.

Over the course of the year, we worked to provide Robert and all our children with a toehold and "way in" to the social involvement and academic learning in our room. When we planned together in August, John and I were determined to emphasize cooperative small groups, student talk and socialization, open-ended activities, and opportunities for children's out-of-school interests and talents. All this was the "social glue" for motivating our students both to be themselves and venture into new ways of thinking and doing and feeling through our first-grade curriculum and activities.

This shared philosophy was also the "professional glue" keeping our co-teaching partnership together—seeing our community-based classroom come to fruition kept John and me going as a team through challenging times. It kept us talking, communicating, and working together. The researcher's study, with its focus on Robert's life in our classroom, challenged us to reaffirm the foundation of our classroom and our teaching partnership.

In November, John and I still hadn't secured extra services for Robert, and his difficulty focusing on work and interactional difficulties with others continued. At the time, Robert began swearing and showing the middle finger to other children. He didn't realize what he was doing, just copying words and actions from other children, but he knew it bothered his peers. On occasion, other children goaded Robert into getting angry and swearing; sometimes Robert did it of his own volition. These episodes bothered all of us, adding a new form of disruption at a time when that was the last thing we needed as a classroom community.

One afternoon, John reached his limit of tolerance; he suspended Robert from school for two days for swearing and flipping other children off. He felt it was getting out of control. Two weeks later, just before Thanksgiving, I suspended Robert for the same thing. I walked Robert to the office, filled out the suspension form (checked the box for the offense of swearing), left it for Marian to sign, and Cindy later called Mrs. Pollard, who came to school and picked up Robert. Mrs. Pollard didn't come to the classroom to talk with me, nor did I call her that day. Partly, I didn't know what to say; it was the first time I had ever suspended a student, and I didn't feel good about it. I was actually having a good day with the class, and the suspension wasn't the common case of losing control of the class and taking it out on individual students like Robert. Rather, as I thought about the meaning of the suspension, I saw that John and I had already formed a perception that Robert stood apart from the rest of the class—and that we therefore needed to "deal" with his difficulties in a different way.

Robert was not the only student we suspended during the year. We did so a few times for offenses such as repeated hitting and swearing. The suspensions, though, seemed to have little effect on decreasing or eliminating the behaviors. Suspensions, from both classroom and school, have powerful ramifications for the already sensitive relationships between teachers, administrators, children, and their families. And the situation can become more charged given the historically disproportionate number of students of color suspended from school. Our district's suspension form had a checklist to indicate children's ethnicity so that the district could keep track of suspension rates. Based on the four or five suspensions John and I gave, we maintained the historical trend. One underlying difficulty for many teachers, as it was for us, is a lack of resources and options for helping children in need of behavioral, personal, and academic assistance. Given the scarcity of extra school personnel, the busy schedules of administrators, large class sizes, and distant relationships with parents, suspensions and other forms of discipline such as detention become used by teachers in a kind of act of desperation.

In a testament to the resiliency of children, the power of the peer world, and the attractions of our classroom, Robert never gave up on finding a place and home in our classroom community. Like all our students, Robert just wanted to have a friend.

Early one May morning Carl and his father, Jeffrey, entered the classroom. The previous day, Jeffrey told me, Carl came home complaining that Robert ate Carl's lunch. I told Jeffrey that it was true, but that I hadn't had time to call home and tell him. The previous day, early in the morning, Carl told me that Robert ate some of his bag lunch, which he left in the back of the room by the jackets. At the time, though, things were so chaotic in the classroom that I couldn't deal with the problem. Later in the morning, though, as I read with one of the literature groups at the horseshoe table, I noticed Robert and Joey doing something under the table. When I looked over, they returned the glance and I knew they were up to something. I walked over and they were eating what appeared to be the rest of Carl's lunch. I took the chips and drink away from Robert. He said it was his, but it was the same food that Carl said he had in his lunch.

At that moment, as I took the lunch, I saw Robert's taking and sharing of Carl's lunch as another thing Robert wasn't supposed to do; I saw it as misbehavior and so I took the food without asking. Writing in my journal later,

I stepped back from my rush to play police officer and authority figure, and I considered Robert's motives. I saw Robert using the chips and drink to become better friends with Joey, a popular and confident member of the boys' peer world and someone who sometimes clashed with Robert. It made sense; better to win Joey over with treats than to confront or challenge him. It was the smart and brave thing to do, for Robert to go out on a limb to be Joey's friend.

In the same journal entry, I recounted another scene from the same morning. As I sat on the rug with the class for morning meeting, I mentioned we "just might" have an earthquake drill and reminded the children of the procedure. In classic first-grade style, several children personalized the topic by recounting their personal experiences of the huge earthquake that had jolted the San Francisco Bay area. Amanda said her house rocked back and forth. Michele said she could see the fires lighting up the sky after the quake. Joey, ever the teller of tall tales, said his house caught fire and they had to evacuate. The children looked wide-eyed. Galen gave a long anecdote about being at a fair when the earthquake hit and seeing the Teenage Mutant Ninja Turtles. With mention of the Turtles, the topic shifted. Like reporters at a news conference, several boys shouted, "Did you see Michelangelo?" "Did you see Donatello?" "Oh, that'd be cool. I wish I could have seen him!" "Did you get to touch any of them?"

Lost in the hubbub of Turtle euphoria was Robert, who chimed in with "Was April there?" April was the television reporter who helped rescue, shelter, and feed the pizza-loving Turtles upon their arrival aboveground from the sewers. I was struck by Robert's question. Not only was it different from the others, it showed engagement with the immensely popular media characters and comprehension of a central character in the Turtle saga. I also noticed that no one picked up on Robert's question. But Robert didn't seem to mind; he seemed satisfied to have made his contribution.

Back in September, it was Robert who initially introduced the Turtles to our classroom. In his first journal entry, Robert drew a figure with a rounded head and long legs and long arms. Robert outlined the pencil marks in orange, purple, and green crayon. The figure's arm moved across the page toward another person, outlined with orange crayon and shaded with purple and brown. Robert wrote "Ol nettRL" on the first line and "Fit" on the next. When John walked by Robert, he asked Robert to "read back" what he wrote.

"The Turtles are fighting," he said.

John responded by writing, "Why do the Turtles fight?"

"They just do!" Robert said with a shrug.

Robert started off the year engaged and involved in some of his work, especially journal writing. In his second entry, Robert wrote "DOALc" for his single line of text. He wrote his name clearly and legibly on top and drew several purple, yellow, blue, and red lines intersecting to make a figure. After he told John that "I'm watching *Reading Rainbow*," John responded by writing, "I love to watch *Reading Rainbow*. Do you?"

In his third entry, Robert drew a Humpty-Dumpty–like figure surrounded by red and purple circles and the first three letters of his name. For his text, Robert wrote "neneo" on line one, "noe hopnenenen" on line two, and "heonnenehinent" on the next line. With Belva beside him, Robert interpreted his work as "I'm walking." Belva responded by writing, "Are you walking to school?" Robert nodded and grinned. Two days later, Robert drew two boxes, one green and blue, and added two small green figures holding hands in the top box. Below his text of "nenene KROTo," Belva responded by writing, "I am the oldest kid in my family, too. I am glad you can ride a bike."

These entries show how Robert participated in one critical academic activity with a degree of success. Robert had a beginning awareness that both pictures and symbols "say" something and can be used to convey information and meaning. Robert, like others in our room, delighted in writing repeated strings of letter patterns like "nenene," which indicates an early experimentation with letters and letter forms. Robert's drawings also reveal an active tinkering with color and shape.

Other classroom activities, though, proved frustrating for Robert. When we made patterns in math, we started with simple "ABABAB" patterns and then the more complex "AABAABAAB" and other variations. We replicated the patterns by clapping hands and snapping fingers, and arranging math manipulatives and then recording the patterns with drawings and cutting and gluing shapes. Robert had an easier time replicating the patterns by clapping or moving objects than recording and representing on paper. In one set of pattern worksheets I created, Robert struggled first to recognize and then continue the printed patterns. The first sheet asked the children to continue "ABAB," "CDCD," and "EFEF" patterns by writing the appropriate letters across a row of boxes.

After I explained the sheet to my small group, I noticed Robert coloring the A's and B's already on the page. I redirected him by showing Robert how to identify the letters, say and repeat the basic pattern, and then write the letters to continue the pattern. For the second pattern, Robert independently wrote "DICDK" (rather than "CDCD") and "FFF" (rather than "EFEF") for the third. I helped Robert break down the task into more manageable pieces to finish the sheet, but Robert appeared to only partially understand. Robert did not entirely "get" the activity, but he was determined to "do" it and finish alongside his tablemates. Showing the power of the peer group and Robert's desire to be included, he didn't want to be left out of doing the work. On page two of the patterns, I realized that five sheets of different kinds of patterns were too taxing for Robert, and at this point I encouraged him to color as he wished in order "to finish" along with the others.

This pattern scene showed me that manipulating actual materials rather than drawing objects was a better way for Robert to understand a traditional math focus such as patterns. Worksheets and representations on paper, even after work with math manipulatives and objects, only served to make the abstract more abstract. The scene also showed how close, individual attention helped Robert and give him the feeling of social–academic inclusion with his tablemates.

John and I and Belva couldn't, and shouldn't, have been at Robert's side all the time. It was thus a daily challenge for Robert to "make it" both academically and socially. On too many occasions over the course of the year, before John and I knew what was happening, some mini-calamity would involve Robert.

One day, Robert raced to morning recess carrying a red rubber ball. He loved the ball, loved to kick it high, watch it soar, and then run to catch it on the bounce. As I watched Robert kick the ball up into the sunny morning, I saw Keith at his side, also wanting the ball. As the two boys gave chase, Keith pushed Robert, who tripped and fell face forward, sliding along the asphalt on his cheek. Robert cried and cried. I rushed to his side and held him as a circle of children gathered. Keith came over and put his arm around Robert. I thanked him but told him to go sit on the bench for a time-out. I unsuccessfully tried to calm Robert. He cried uncontrollably. I then half-carried Robert to the office, where Cindy bandaged his cuts. I filled out the accident report and called Mrs. Pollard. She wasn't upset about the injury and thanked me for calling. She came to get Robert, and he remained out of school for over a week. I had Keith write Robert a letter of apology and draw a picture. The letter was quite beautiful; Keith said he was sorry and hoped Robert would forgive him.

When Robert returned to school, he was the first to arrive in the morning. He had two large scabs on his cheek. I welcomed him back and asked if he wanted to help me take the chairs down from the tables. Although Robert often was the first to arrive, this was the first time I had invited him to stay in the room with me before the start of school; Robert's fall brought me closer to him. Robert cheerfully took down the chairs. I then suggested that later on he could write a letter to Irene, the special education aide helping him. Robert walked to the writing center and placed an envelope and paper on the table. Later during morning meeting, I had Robert draw a picture and put the letter in the envelope. He asked if he could bring the letter downstairs to Irene. I said yes. With a big grin, off he went on his special errand.

Even as Robert experienced interactional difficulties with children at recess and in the hallways, gaining a schoolwide reputation, he managed to make positive connections with other adults at Mayfield. Robert loved Cora, our downstairs first-grade colleague. He'd drop by her room, stand in the doorway, and hope for a smile or a wave and a "How's my little friend doing?"

from her. Robert would smile with pride. He often slipped into last place in our line after recess or lunch, and as I turned around on the stairs, I saw him sneak toward Cora's door.

Robert also loved going next door to Doris's third-grade class. Doris didn't mind and offered to take Robert "anytime." One day, I turned around in class and noticed Robert missing. I started to panic. I checked Doris's room, and there sat Robert in the middle of the third graders, smiling and loving the attention and the calm of the classroom. I let him stay. Robert disappeared again on another day. This time I located him downstairs in the special education classroom for children with physical disabilities. Robert sat in the teacher's rocking chair, strumming a guitar and having a great time.

To add to what he had in our classroom, Robert added a special hug from Cora, special time hanging out with the third graders, and the comforting rhythm of the rocking chair and the music of the guitar.

In September, we informed Marian of our concerns about Robert. She asked us to fill out a Student Study Team (SST) form to start the process of seeking additional services for Robert. We filled out the form and Marian scheduled a meeting for the first week of October. As we gathered in the faculty lounge for the meeting, we learned that Mrs. Pollard had just called the office to cancel. Marian suggested we proceed anyway since Roger, the school psychologist; Joan, the school's resource specialist; and Antoinette, the school's nurse all only came to Mayfield one or two days a week.

We discussed and filled in the categories listed on the SST chart: Strengths, Known Information, Concerns, Modifications, Plan of Action, Persons Responsible, and Timetable. Marian pointed out that the chart starts with strengths in order to emphasize the child's positive qualities. John and I talked about what we knew about Robert, detailing his major strengths and weaknesses and referring to specific examples of his behavior and samples of his work we'd brought. We emphasized that Robert needed extra services and needed them soon.

After completing the chart, which did provide a balanced and comprehensive view of Robert, we discussed possible services for Robert. Roger explained that while Robert had been in a special day class before, it didn't mean that we could just place him in one again; Mrs. Pollard had to approve, and Roger had to carry out a battery of tests to determine Robert's eligibility. In the meantime, we asked Roger, what could we do for Robert in the classroom? Roger said that he'd come observe next week. Marian said she'd schedule another SST meeting so that Mrs. Pollard could come. John and I left the meeting frustrated that all wasn't settled; we wanted a clear and set plan for getting extra help both for Robert and ourselves.

Two weeks later, Marian sent us a note that Mrs. Pollard couldn't attend the rescheduled meeting. Mrs. Pollard told Marian that she didn't want the special day class at another school for Robert, but agreed to Mayfield's resource specialist program. The meeting was rescheduled for the first week of November. John and I were disappointed that Mrs. Pollard had to reschedule and didn't want the special day class.

Mrs. Pollard came to the next meeting. We gathered in the staff lounge. Marian raised the issue of the special day class again. Mrs. Pollard described what it had previously been like for Robert in a special day class. Children in the class were "very troubled" and exhibited odd behaviors, which Robert only imitated. She considered it a poor placement for Robert and didn't want to repeat it. I understood Mrs. Pollard's concern; I pictured Robert in the special day class, imitating other children's behavior just as he did in our class.

Mrs. Pollard thought Robert's primary problem in paying attention and focusing was due to hyperactivity. John and I agreed that Robert had a lot of energy, but we also described the extent to which concepts and curriculum content were hard and frustrating for Robert. Mrs. Pollard said that Robert's previous year in a private school had helped and he was less hyperactive. Antoinette, the school nurse, mentioned that eye tests in September had shown that Robert had astigmatism. She also suggested that Robert could receive outside testing from a local children's hospital. Mrs. Pollard said that she had looked into that possibility, but couldn't do it just yet because she was changing health insurance.

It was finally decided that Robert would receive extra help from the school's resource program. Joan said that Irene, her special education instructional aide, would work with Robert for 15 to 30 minutes each day. Roger said that the remainder of the special education referral and testing process would take 50 calendar days to complete, which pushed the date into January. Once he completed testing, which required Mrs. Pollard's approval, Roger would schedule an Individualized Educational Plan (IEP) meeting for Robert. Roger would inform us of the date.

Irene worked with Robert from 10:20 to 10:45 every day. She was wonderful, and Robert loved her. Irene started Robert on a reading program on the computer in her room downstairs and rewarded Robert with stickers and small toys. Robert always wanted to "go downstairs and see Irene." When he returned with a whistle or a balloon as a prize, he loved parading his trophies, preening with pride and accomplishment. John and I were glad for the help, and pleased to see Robert's pleasure in working with Irene.

Robert's IEP meeting was scheduled for February 7. On the day, Mrs. Pollard called to say she couldn't make it. Roger later called and obtained Mrs. Pollard's verbal permission to test Robert. In February, and then again in April, Roger gave Robert a battery of tests as part of the required "psycho-educational evaluation." Once testing was complete, Roger scheduled an IEP meeting for April 26th. At the meeting, based on a battery of 10 tests assessing such areas as "knowledge of verbal concepts" and Robert's "level of visual perception," Roger concluded that all the test results "fell significantly below age level and below Robert's present first-grade placement." Roger made several recommendations, including completing "a structured interview around development and socialization" with Mrs. Pollard, "creating a cognitive behavior modification plan" for the classroom, and "setting up chores so that Robert can see himself as helpful and capable of doing things in school." Roger added that he would draw up an IEP once he completed one last test with Mrs. Pollard. It was almost May, though, and Roger and Mrs. Pollard never did meet to complete the IEP.

In the second week of March, Robert was selected as our Student of the Week. He had waited seven months for the honor, and he wasn't disappointed. It was the best five consecutive days of his first-grade experience. Robert loved standing in front as line leader, loved taking the ball out for morning recess, loved the Student of the Week interview, loved receiving a letter from each child, loved choosing two children to help color and cut out a life-size version of his body on butcher paper.

During his interview, seated on our big wooden chair, Robert looked out over the children with one of his trademark grins. Having waited so long for this moment of honor and attention, Robert knew exactly what to do. He immediately sat down in the chair, faced the class, and waited for the other children to raise their hands so he could call on them. Over the year, we taught the children first to ask "information" questions such as, "How old are you?," "Do you have any brothers and sisters?," and "Where do you live?" before "personal" questions such as, "What's your favorite food?" (all the children said pizza), "Your favorite movie?" (*Teenage Mutant Ninja Turtles* was a front-runner), and "What do you want to be when you grow up?" (answers ranged from store manager to lawyer).

Robert had trouble with some of the early questions. Joey asked his age. Robert replied "five." Some children laughed. Others said he couldn't possibly be five and be in first grade. John, sensing a critical moment for Robert during his special week, stepped in. He asked Robert if he wouldn't mind going outside of the classroom for a moment; Robert wasn't in trouble, but John just wanted to talk with the class about their behavior. The children sat quietly and attentively; they too sensed the importance of the moment. John explained that it was hard for Robert to answer some of the questions exactly right, but they could not make fun of him. Then John continued.

In a rare kind of honest conversation between children and teachers, John said that he knew Robert could be a hard kid to get along with, and that John himself had contributed to this perception and was guilty of adding to the problem. He added that everybody in our class, adults included, had their own particular strengths and weaknesses and that Robert had certain difficulties and strengths learning and doing things in school. He and the children talked some more, and Robert returned to finish the interview without further incident.

When John told me what had happened, I couldn't believe it. John said that he hadn't planned on such a talk; it just seemed the right thing to do, and wished we'd done it much earlier in the year. So bent on seeking extra outside services for Robert, John and I had lost track of our own ability to turn things around for Robert in our classroom. It may not have been the "textbook" thing for John to do, but an honest, two-way discussion gave some voice to one child's experience of our classroom.

Two weeks before the end of the school year, all three first-grade classes boarded a big yellow school bus for a trip to a nearby beach. I sat next to Robert on the bus. He loved the bus. Robert loved the way it moved, the breeze through the windows, the scenery outside. Robert asked what kind of bus it was. "A school bus," I said. It tickled him. Every few minutes or so, he played the game of asking, "What kind of bus is this?" and delighted himself in answering, "A school bus!"

Robert had a wonderful time at the beach. He didn't bring a swimsuit, but entertained himself by playing with a ball, bouncing it against a slanted wall and catching it on the rebound. At one point, I noticed Robert leave the wall and walk way down the beach, playing with children from other school groups and sipping their cans of soda pop as he went. Robert had a glorious day.

The following week, all classes at Mayfield went on the annual end-of-the-year picnic at a park in a nearby city. I again sat next to Robert on the bus and again played the name-the-bus game, Robert still enraptured with the rollicking and bumping bus. As on the beach trip, Robert had no problems with other children during the three hours at the park. Toward the end of the trip, I reached into my pocket and pulled out Robert's folded, crinkled permission slip for the trip. When Robert handed me the slip earlier in the morning, I was rushed and assumed that Mrs. Pollard had signed it. Unfolding the paper at the park, I looked for Mrs. Pollard's signature. It wasn't there. Only a row of letters in Robert's handwriting. I laughed. I held up the paper and shouted for John. I handed him the slip of paper. John looked at it.

"Robert fooled us," he said.

"He sure did," I said with a laugh.

In September, as in the beginning of any human relationship, the participants in our classroom had the opportunity to create ourselves anew. We could be someone we weren't, make ourselves up; we didn't know each other. But salient bits and pieces of our identities were evident from our first moments together. We couldn't hide. As we carried on each day, for 181 days, we learned each other's foibles and strengths. When weaknesses and areas of difficulty rose to the surface and became public, as happened with Robert and others, John and I learned that we needed to address the overall issue of individual differences and work as a classroom community to help each other feel accepted.

For beginning as well as more experienced teachers, though, recognizing and helping individual students in need is one of the biggest challenges in teaching. It involves a keen sense of observation—seeing and hearing and feeling—beyond simple identification of students as "at risk" or "underachieving" or in need of "early intervention." It also requires, as John and I learned in our year-long efforts to help Robert, that teachers can't wait for outside support to arrive. Teachers have to rely on their ready wits and bag of tricks, or if nothing else their inner conviction in the strengths and positive aspects of their classroom, until help comes. And if assistance doesn't arrive as hoped for, as John and I experienced, it becomes even more imperative to maintain a positive outlook and an ongoing reserve of patient energy.

After all, what Robert wanted and what Robert deserved was simple and understandable—he only wanted to "play soccer and swing on the tire swing" and "sit down and do work." It is also important, as John and I learned, to avoid the inclination to "deal" with rather than *teach* children in need of extra help—it only adds to everyone's feeling of separateness. And when teachers and children grow too far apart, teachers' teaching instincts and children's attachments to each other and the curriculum can't work their full influence. The fight, then, is to keep moving toward closeness and connection, and to learn from the little events and scenes with individual children.

10

"Am I going to repeat?"–
Testing and Teaching

<u>What I Love</u>

I love TV because it is fun. I like the funny shows.

by Carl

Teachers should at all times exhibit proper animation themselves, manifesting a lively interest in the subject taught; avoid all heavy, plodding movements, all formal routine in teaching, lest the pupil be dull and drowsy, and imbibe the notion that he studies only to recite.

"Instructions to Teachers,"
California Public School Register, 1891

Like an upside-down cake, important perceptions of both student and teacher success are influenced by the small measures of standardized tests and formal teacher evaluations. Involving children, teachers, administrators, parents, and community members, testing and assessment in schools touch an array of politically and educationally sensitive issues and concerns. During the second half of the school year, John and I experienced and confronted some of these issues. As new teachers at Mayfield and in the district, John and I were evaluated by our site administrator, Marian, and we also administered standardized tests to our students.

John and I were wary of a formal evaluation of our teaching. Even with improvements in our classroom organization and curriculum, John and I knew we needed to do better. We were new teachers, and John and I wanted to do well on our first go-round, and show ourselves, our colleagues, and the Mayfield community that we were competent and skilled teachers—and we felt that testing played a role in these early perceptions.

Marian told us that she would conduct a formal observation, complete an evaluation form, and meet with us to discuss her observation. I arranged for Marian to observe me on February 20. Given the advance notice, I tried to stay relaxed and not worry about how things would go. During the observation, we worked in our usual morning literature groups as I sat with the 49ers and taught an activity based on Arnold Lobel's *Mouse Soup.* We had read the book for the past few days, and I led the group in a discussion of the "Wishing Well" story. I asked the children what they would wish for if they had three magic wishes.

"A new bicycle."

"A million dollars."

"A new Turtle set."

"Another wish."

I then held up a piece of paper with a picture of a wishing well, and said that I wanted the children to write their own "wishing story." I showed them where to write and draw on the sheet. The activity went well; the children knew the story, liked it, and found the writing and drawing engaging. In addition, we were all in a good mood that morning, and the activity flowed along as if it were an everyday occurrence.

I met Marian later in her office to discuss her visit. She handed me a form entitled "Instrument for the Formal Observation of Teaching Activities."

Under "What was the objective of the lesson (i.e., what was to be learned?)," Marian noted:

> Reading *Mouse Soup*
> Writing in journals
> Reading cartoons from a newspaper and creating their own cartoon
>   characters
> Retelling *Mouse Soup* in writing or writing their own version
> Free choice time—the use of Legos

For "What was the student to do to demonstrate or give 'feedback' to the teacher that he had learned?," Marian wrote:

> Students were to read *Mouse Soup* with the teacher
> Write in journals or on paper wishing wells
> Complete cartoon pictures and make dialogue bubbles to write in

"Was this lesson appropriate for the learners (i.e., not too easy, building on something they knew, challenging but not overwhelming)?"

> Yes

"What did the teacher do to facilitate learning? How did he or she utilize learning theory of motivation, reinforcement, retention, and conceptualization? Were directions clear? Were the instructional materials suitable?"

> Activities were motivating to the students
> Verbal praise was used

"What did the teacher do that interfered with learning?"

> Nothing

For "Teacher's strengths observed," Marian noted "a variety of reading/language arts activities taking place" and left the "teacher's weaknesses observed" section empty. At the end of the form, in the small space for "other concepts and suggestions by the principal or evaluator," Marian noted "evidence that science, social studies, writing, and literature are valued. Students were on task and proud of their work." I elected to leave the "comments by teacher" space empty and signed and dated the form.

Walking out of Marian's office, holding the Xeroxed evaluation, I felt like I had passed a mini-test of my first year teaching at Mayfield. Only later did I realize the pressure that the formal evaluation had placed on me, and how more frequent and ongoing observations throughout the year would help improve my teaching. Like the need to restructure the district's once-a-year parent–teacher conferences, the district's teacher evaluations needed to be changed. With more contact and more opportunities for dialogue, teachers and administrators will have a more genuine, ongoing forum for discussing and critiquing the day-to-day details of teaching and learning in classrooms. It will help avoid teacher evaluation as a once- or twice-a-year bureaucratic dance between administrator and teacher, and promote engaging and critical discussions about the here-and-now of teaching.

A few days after my evaluation meeting with Marian, local newspapers reported low test scores for two out of three subjects on the California Assessment Program for third, six, eighth, and twelfth graders in our district. The articles noted two schools, including Mayfield, with particularly low scores for third graders. Our district school board members publicly voiced their concerns with the low test scores. One member thought the preponderance of heterogeneous grouping practices in the district kept back bright students, and that monies spent on special needs and at-risk students needed to shift to average and above-average students. A testing controversy then ensued over the next several weeks, causing a flurry of reaction and counter-reaction from parents, teachers, administrators, and board members at Mayfield and throughout the district.

At Mayfield, we were particularly hurt by the lingering perception that poor teaching was partially to blame for our low test scores. We drafted letters to the school board to voice our disagreement, and a number of our parents supported us with letters and phone calls to the board. Our faculty felt that the district's test score presentation to the board was not accompanied by a thoughtful analysis of the complicated factors underlying standardized test results. Meeting as an entire staff, we agreed on a list of suggestions to improve test scores: student populations to be equally distributed, extra district resources to respond to each school's need, lower class sizes, and more instructional aides for classrooms. We invited district administrators and school board members to discuss these and other matters with us.

One school board member accepted. Meeting with our staff, the board member told us that teachers do play a critical role in student learning, and highlighted the importance of additional resources and structural changes to improve test scores and the academic achievement of students of color in particular. Our staff agreed, and we spent the remaining time discussing how we could work with the board and district administration to improve the academic achievement of our lowest-achieving students. We were pleased that our voices were heard. But as often happens when test scores are reported, there is a sudden rush to find the root causes and ideas for improvement are bandied about, but then no firm and tangible changes are agreed upon and implemented in a concerted manner over a period of time.

The testing controversy foreshadowed an annual rite of spring in schools: standardized testing. John and I were required to administer the Comprehensive Test of Basic Skills (CTBS) in May. In our staff meetings and Marian's newsletters to the staff and parent body, the upcoming testing received a great deal of attention. In late May, Marian informed us in a staff bulletin that "CTBS materials will be distributed today. I encourage you to test half the class at a time. Detailed instructions regarding activities in the auditorium and on the playground (for the half of the class not tested) will be in your box on Monday morning."

Marian also listed a number of caveats and reminders:

- Please read the test manual and become familiar with the format, sequence and timing of the test
- Directions should be read exactly as written
- Testing should take place in the morning only
- Bells will be turned off in the morning—until 12:00
- Provide the best possible test situation. Be careful not to reward those who finish quickly by allowing them to leave the room or do special things
- Scratch/drawing paper and books to read for the ones who finish quickly should be available before the testing begins
- Cardboard dividers prevent problems of "looking at others' tests"

Marian added that the "PTA is donating $200.00 worth of fruit as a snack for testing. It will be delivered either Monday afternoon or Tuesday morning."

An April 11 parent newsletter informed all Mayfield families that "we are now preparing our students to take the annual Comprehensive Test of Basic Skills (CTBS) which will be given from April 30th to May 3rd. The CTBS test measures a child's achievement in reading, language, and math at his/her grade level. A week before the test we will send more suggestions regarding how to make sure your child will do his/her best on the test."

Marian suggested we practice test-taking procedures with our students before official testing. During the last two weeks in April, I had the children work on Xeroxed pages of a practice test booklet. I called it playing the "bubble game." The children, though, thought it anything but a game. Although a few enjoyed mushing their pencil points into the bubbles until they tore holes in the paper, most children disliked it. I did too; it was little fun to exhort our students to do a new kind of activity many found dull and defeating.

John didn't want to do any practice work. He strongly disagreed with the standardized testing of children, though he said he'd administer the tests because he "had to." Recalling his own educational experiences, John said that standardized and other kinds of formal tests had placed him in the lowest math and reading groups as a child and he had felt like a social and academic outcast, and he argued that elements of such tests are culturally biased. In addition, he said, the tests aren't helpful in helping teachers learn more about children's individual strengths and weaknesses, and thus aren't helpful in improving the quality and effectiveness of teaching. I told John that while I didn't share his personal memories of being tracked into low groups as a child, and I agreed with him on the issue of cultural bias, I pointed out that we would do our students a disservice by not helping them prepare for the inevitability of testing.

The practice test questions were difficult; they asked our students to think both conceptually and procedurally in ways John and I hadn't emphasized over the previous eight months. In Lesson 1 of the practice word analysis section, the directions stated, "Turn to page 3. Look at the four words in row 1. Mark under the word that begins with same sound as *boy*, *boy*." The children then had to find the corresponding beginning sound in "did," "bad," "fun," or "got." John and I did little isolated skill work in decoding words or computing mathematical equations on paper without the use of manipulatives and objects. Although I used more worksheets than John, they more closely resembled the Arnold Lobel "Wishing Well" activity than the bubble items on the practice tests.

John and I were ambivalent about administering the tests, and yet we were aware of our colleagues' practice testing and the general schoolwide expectation that the tests mattered. John and I felt in a bind; we didn't place much educational value on the tests, yet we wanted our children to do well and we didn't want low test scores to reflect badly on our teaching. As professionals, playing the "bubble game" made John and I feel that we lacked control, direction, and power over our own teaching and our students' learning. By the spring, after the cumulative ups and downs of the previous several months, John and I wanted concrete confirmation that we had done a good job teaching our first graders. We wanted to end the year feeling good about ourselves and our co-teaching year. The impending tests were not the kind of confirmation we had in mind.

On the eve of the testing, Marian sent home a list of "tips for parents." For "the night before the test provide your child with sufficient sleep," "consider talking about the test to reassure and encourage your child. At the same time, don't dwell on the subject, as you may cause your child to worry unnecessarily." For the "morning of the test have your child get up early without hurrying, have your child eat a good breakfast, and be positive when you send your child to school."

We started testing the next day, and thank goodness for the PTA snacks. John and I didn't wait until we finished administering each subtest before handing out apple drinks and boxes of raisins and fruit roll-ups. Out they went right along with directions to "put your finger on the box" and "which shape looks exactly like the one in the box." Our children sensed that our admonishments to "do your own work" and "not to talk" and "not look at your neighbor's work" signaled an unfamiliar way of working and interacting. They were also aware that life in the entire school was not normal—during testing week, bells stopped, doors were closed with signs noting "Shhh! Testing!," and we were to walk quietly at all times in the hallways.

Before starting the testing, I gave a pregame pep talk to our class. I stood in the middle of the room, test booklets and special No. 2 pencils in hand, as the children sat away from each other at desks and tables. I said that John and I were proud of the children, that they had worked hard all year long and had learned a lot. I added that some of the things on the tests would be hard and some easy. I encouraged them to try their best and work hard. Whatever happened, I said, they were all learning in their own ways and at their own pace. Scanning their faces, I saw the same kind of puzzled expression as when I explained our shared teaching schedule on the first day of school.

Even before testing started, students had difficulty—they wrote their names on the front of the booklets, opened their booklets without waiting, and broke their pencil tips from pressing too hard. Altering our accustomed pattern of instruction, John and I proceeded with the testing in lockstep fashion—telling, explaining, doing, checking. Verbatim direction by verbatim direction from the test instruction manual, subtest by subtest, item by item, bubble by bubble, frown by frown. Off we went.

On the whole, our students had a terrible time of it. Not only did our less experienced readers have difficulty with many of the test items, so did our more experienced readers like Amanda and Michele and Warren. Although the math went more easily than the reading, it was a generally painful few days of testing. John and I disliked it all the more as we went, but on we plodded with the seven subtests.

I ended the first day of testing with a headache. At home, I recorded the day's testing scenes in my journal.

There have been tears, fidgeting, pleas to go to the bathroom, tearing of paper and hair, putting heads down in resignation, talking out, attempts at cheating, hard work, and beautiful Teenage Mutant Ninja Turtles made here and there during the testing. I had the 49ers and the A's stay in the room for testing, while the MC Hammers and Raiders went to the playground.

It was hard at first to get them all quiet. I explained that some of the test would be easy, and some really hard like second-grade work. I'm not sure that part went over well. Then I added that the test does not cover everything that John and I had taught, and it also included some things that we didn't teach. But that we wanted the children to try hard and do as best they could.

I said that even John and I had to take tests at graduate school, and as much as we didn't like to take them, we had to. I also said that they would have to take tests for a long time in their educational careers, and it would help to learn some things about taking tests. I added that if they didn't know an answer, they should take a guess— that any try is better than no attempt.

And on I wrote, recalling that the "the first to lose it was Arthur, who began to cry as it soon became apparent that he could hardly read much of what the test was demanding, and also had trouble figuring out what it was that he was supposed to be doing in each question and section."

Arthur "really gave me a run for my money. At one point he blurted out, 'I don't want to fail this test. I want to go to second grade.'" With no time to think, only react, I walked to Arthur and gave him a little hug and whispered that he'd go to second grade. Worried that others felt similar feelings of failure and fear of being retained, I stopped the testing for a moment and told the class that the test had nothing to do with advancing to second grade. In my journal, I wondered if I was "sugarcoating" it all for Arthur and for other students who already had "fail" in their six-year-old vocabularies.

Finished with the first subtest, I passed out fruit roll-ups as I walked the children to the playground. I brought the other half of the class back. In my journal that same night, the testing drama continued.

In the next group, I had Jerome and Joey. Both started crying. Jerome had the biggest tears streaming down his cheeks. First from one eye, and then the other. They just streamed, as he quietly sat and tried to make sense of the test, of what I said, of the whole thing. What a terrible culmination to all the frustrations he has felt this year academically. I felt so bad for him. I got him some tissue and a little pile of Wheat Thins. The tears were coming from his big eyes, down over his long eyelashes, and over and down his cheeks. He recovered, though barely. Joey squirmed and turned and wrestled with himself and the test as if he were having a bad dream. Finally, he put his head down on his arms and cried. I gave him the extra Wheat Thin treatment too.

Our collective testing misery continued the next day. I continued to document the little, personal scenes behind the impersonal, distant nature of the tests, with which we found little worthwhile social or academic connection.

On Wednesday, Gina started crying. I finally told the whole class that they just could make a mark on each problem and take a guess, that it was alright and it was the best thing to do. How sad the whole thing is for most of the kids. Some, like Janet and Matthew, didn't seem affected, and they actually tried to read all of the test! It took them forever though, and I had to cut some of their work short. Even Amanda and Warren, our two best readers, became frustrated. Warren started crying during the section where you have to choose the sentences with the correct punctuation, and Amanda became frustrated on the section where she had to read a very long (about fourteen lines) story on her own and then answer comprehension questions based on the story.

For the rest of testing, I continued doling out the PTA rations and more and more scratch paper, and noticed the children's creative efforts during testing.

I gave out scratch paper for the kids to draw on while they waited for others to finish the subtest yesterday. Galen and Keith and Jerome drew and worked on detailed and intricate Turtles. Amanda wrote a one-page story about an old lady, and she wanted to take her story outside to the playground to finish it. Kimberly and Nicole wanted crayons to use in their pictures, but I didn't want them to mark their test books with crayon. We finished the testing on Thursday. A tough couple of days. I'll have to get them some cookies for tomorrow!

Before morning meeting the next day, Jerome asked, "Are we still doing those tests?"

"No," I said. "We're all done."

He smiled one of his biggest smiles of the year.

John and I sent a note home to our families regarding the testing: "CTBS testing is over as of today! It has been a hard and strenuous three days for many children. Please give your child an extra pat on the back! They deserve it, for they tried hard with a difficult test."

We received our class test scores a month later, two weeks before the end of the school year in mid-June. Like students receiving their grades in the mail, John and I pulled the long, computer-generated score sheets from our mailboxes in the teachers' workroom.

"They don't mean much, Dan," John said with reassurance. "We know what our kids can do. And anyway," he added with a wink, "we all know that the tests are culturally biased."

At home that evening, I added a coda to the testing saga.

> Ah yes, how could I forget? We got our test scores back today. We did pretty awful. One did really well, and some of the others did OK. But even our great readers did poorly. Much of the class was pretty low. Pretty depressing. All that fuss and what not over those tests. What a waste of time, energy, and money. Hope if we're back next year, that we won't do them again.

At first glance, the computer printout of the scores was a dizzying array of numbers. From left to right, the "Class Record Sheet" listed tests for Reading (with subtests of vocabulary and comprehension), Language (mechanics and expression), Mathematics (computation and concepts/application), Total Battery, and Word Analysis. The key at the bottom of the page explained the five scores: MDNP for "median national percentile," MNS for "mean national stanine," GME for "grade mean equivalent," MNCE for "mean normal curve equivalent," and MSS for "mean scale score."

In each individual student report, a note to parents stated that "the test results give you information about your child's level of achievement at the time of testing. A bar graph shows the scores for each test taken. At the bottom of the page is a comparison of test scores for reading, language, and mathematics, with 1st grade results nationally." The horizontal bar graph listed student results for the subtests and tests. The graph scale showed a range divided into "below average," "average" (shaded gray), and "above average." Three boxes below for "Reading," "Language," and "Mathematics" explained the bar graph results. For Reading, the box explained one student's test scores in comparison with national results: "Your child scored higher than 6% of all 1st grade students in the nation in Total Reading. Reading Vocabulary was higher than 6%; Reading Comprehension was higher than 6%."

Our whole-class profile indicated mean national percentiles for Reading as 10.0, Language 11.0, Mathematics 21.0, Word Analysis 22.0, and the Total Battery 14.5. Pretty low. Only a few students scored in the average to above average range: one student scored in the 99th percentile for Reading, 87.0

for Language, and 86.0 for Mathematics; another 61.0 for Reading, 32.0 for Language, and 49.0 for Mathematics; another 52.0 for Reading, 35.0 for Language, and 71.0 for Mathematics. The rest of our class, the majority, showed percentile scores in the below average range.

John and I were embarrassed to send the scores home to our families. We wanted our students to do well, we wanted our families to be proud of their children, and we wanted our families to perceive us as excellent teachers. We hoped they wouldn't place too much stock in the scores. John and I included the scores along with the final report card, which we handed out on the last day of school, and hoped parents wouldn't question us. They didn't.

The standardized tests and report cards were district-wide tools for student assessment and documentation. They were intended to cut across individual differences, language and cultural backgrounds, and variation in teaching philosophies, styles, and methods. And yet, as John and I experienced, testing has the potential power to touch and influence our most sensitive and personal feelings of self-worth as children, teachers, and participants in schools and communities. We were all in it together, each tied to each other's strengths and weaknesses, the test results indicating something about each one of us.

The testing was a "bubble game," but one that had the powerful potential to influence perceptions of how well John and I taught and how well our students learned. Seeing our students working on the tests, John and I had first-hand evidence of how some children at age six already have strong perceptions about the role of tests during their early school years. And in a complementary way, the tests also represented a potentially powerful indicator of our effectiveness as new teachers at Mayfield and in the district. Just as Arthur and Gina wanted to do well and not be outside their peer group, John and I wanted to remain within *our* peer group of colleagues. Just as the children didn't want to be left out and Arthur wanted to go on to second grade, John and I didn't want to be left out; we wanted to end the year feeling successful and competent.

In our staff development training and graduate school work, John and I were introduced to "alternative forms of assessment" such as portfolios and ongoing observations of student learning. In our teacher education texts and workshops, these new assessment tools were presented as ways to improve on traditional standardized tests because of their closer connection to actual teaching and learning. While John and I liked many of these ideas—particularly journals, learning logs, portfolios, and conferences—like most teachers, we "had to give" standardized tests.

So John and I did. But it was painful for us, our students, and their families. The tests took valuable and hard-earned time and momentum away from our curriculum late in the school year, and gave the children mixed and confusing messages about the kind of educational values and goals that John and

I and the school were trying to promote. Rather than supporting our efforts to create a classroom community based on creativity, sharing, and collegiality, the tests made evident and public the differences in academic performance in our diverse classroom. And yet John and I felt that we came together as a classroom community during the testing; we cooperated with each other, some children even tried to help each other as we had taught them to do, and they shared their rations of fruit roll-ups and raisins. In the process, we saw each other through a common ordeal.

How do teachers know they've done a good job? After seeing the test scores, John and I couldn't help thinking that if our classroom curriculum and structure had been different, our scores would have been higher. During subsequent lunch periods, over tuna sandwiches and cream sodas and big bags of chips, we renewed our testing discussions. John and I revisited the notion that we did our students a disservice by not spending more time on teacher-directed activities and worksheets designed to focus on parts of language and procedures for answering test-like items.

Maybe, we pondered, we should acknowledge the importance of tests as important gatekeepers that students need to conquer to be successful in schools and "make it" in the outside world. Maybe we needed to give our students the tools to beat the tests, to do the "bubble game" and succeed in the world on the terms of the "test makers." John and I found no easy answers as we talked, but at the least our lunchtime debates showed us the continuing personal and professional value of our teaching partnership as we neared the close of our year together. Our partnership continued to provide a safe and lively "place" for voicing and exchanging our feelings and ideas about our own teaching and education.

When I saw Amanda write the one-page story about an old man during our testing, I was both disappointed and pleased. I was disappointed and perplexed at how such a strong reader had a hard time with the reading sections, and wondered where we had gone "wrong" in our language arts instruction, but I was glad to see Amanda write the story and want to finish it at recess. Her story showed me that Amanda's interest in writing, even in moments of academic frustration with the tests, revealed the kind of initiative and creativity that John and I wanted to foster in our students.

A few weeks earlier, John and I had taught a poetry unit with the children. The children loved the poems, rocking to the rhythms and chanting the lines from their favorites. We wrote rain poems one day. I gave the children long pieces of thick pink and magenta paper for their poems, and the children readily took to the activity, commenting on each other's work and chatting as they drew and wrote. They were noisy poets.

Amanda created a lively, multivoiced poem.

1 rain drop 2 rain drop
evey drop is a
happy drop with
a voice like
This. he-he-he
that's why it
is a rain drop
that say's
he-he-he.

Underneath, Amanda drew a line separating her text from several large rain-drops with the words "he-he-he" written in. She added a storm cloud with a carefully designed jagged thunderbolt. I praised Amanda for the poem's sound and movement. I was proud of her.

"Every drop is a happy drop." In the moments of her writing and in the moments of my reading, she and I must have felt something similar—a click-ing of teaching and learning, a meshing of mood and words and literary move-ment in a short, nine-line poem, the kind of literary experience John and I wanted to promote between our students and ourselves. We considered it *good* teaching because it was *our* teaching. No matter Amanda's test scores, Amanda could write a rain poem that moved and talked with a "he-he-he" all the way from the clouds.

11

"You're looking like a little kid"–
Toward a Sense of Closure

My Trip at the Beach

It was fun when I was teasing John. And it was fun to see the
stingray.

by Michele

John and I saw the year's end as a time of leave-taking and parting from the social and intellectual community we had built from the first day of school. Most importantly, we wanted to bring a sense of closure to the complicated set of human relationships formed during our time together. In planning our remaining activities and events, John and I wanted to comfort the children about our imminent good-byes and prepare everyone for the end of our classroom community. We added new activities and revisited old favorites; John and I wanted the children to recall events and activities shared during the year, as well as to recognize and celebrate their learning and growth.

In May and June, events outside our classroom also contributed to an end-of-year sense of community. We went on three field trips. The entire first grade traveled to an aquarium and science museum, then to a sunny beach by the bay, and finally to the annual all-school picnic at a park for a day of games and food. The day before the park trip, the Mayfield community celebrated with an evening "Multicultural Songfest" put on by Cynthia, the new music teacher who had replaced Geoffrey in the spring. Standing on the wing of the stage with my first-grade colleagues, noticing how "old" the children now looked, we waited for Cynthia's cue to sing Bill Brennan's "When My Shoes Are Loose" and the Ghanaian "Che Che Koolay."

In the classroom, John and I kept the children engaged and involved in whole-class projects. In late May, we created a class magazine. Designed as a culminating writing activity, the children wrote and dictated stories that we typed, cut and pasted, and Xeroxed for our students and other classes at Mayfield. The children loved putting together their own personal copies of the magazine, punching holes on the side, choosing colored yarn for binding, and coloring the cover. They took great pride in the magazine, searching for their names listed in the "Table of Contributors," and reading the stories and looking at the drawings. I contributed a word find of all our 30 names at the back of the magazine. Word finds, and hunting for words going "across" and "up and down" and even on the "diagonal," were all the rage with the children at the time. When the children received their magazines, they spread out on the rug, pencil in hand, ready to circle the names in the word find.

The magazine contributions reveal a mini-portrait of the children's growth over the year. Ernesto, who loved drawing and writing about boats, wanted to include a boat from his journal for the magazine and cleverly ripped out the entire journal page. I explained that the drawing must be smaller and in black ink for photocopying; Ernesto, who loved working from models in books and other sources, then copied his journal boat onto a much smaller piece of paper using a black ballpoint pen. I asked him to dictate an accompanying story. In solid English, Ernesto said, "The boat will go into the water. And my father fell down." He paused to look at me. I asked if there was more. "I helped him get up. We went to the mountains in the boat." I asked him how he would get to the mountains by boat, and Ernesto moved his hand back and forth and said, "like this"—a river. Several months after arriving in this country, Ernesto relied on the use of models (pictorial), consistent themes and objects (like boats), and a quiet determination (scaling down the big journal boat onto the small piece of paper) in engaging in his work. His boat story also showed how Ernesto benefited from John's bilingual talents, as John provided Ernesto with a daily dose of academic content and social knowledge in English and Spanish. When they spoke, it was a special connection for both Ernesto and for John, and the rest of the children stopped and looked on at the linguistic interchange.

Dictating his magazine piece, Jerome returned to the jail theme started on the first day of journal writing back in September.

The Bad Boys

There was a bad boy who picked on people, didn't have any lunch money, and at lunch time he stole lots of money to get lunch and then he got taken to jail. Then he was hungry when he got to jail.

The End

He then drew a figure with a tall hat and a frowning, sad face to accompany the story. As I later reread the story, I thought back over Jerome's year in our classroom. I was at first disappointed that John and I had not done more to bolster his academic development, for even at the end of first grade, and it was his second year, too, Jerome didn't feel very successful in his writing. But

I also realized that while John and I had made certain mistakes with Jerome, we had provided ongoing opportunities for Jerome to learn with more consistency and stability.

Amanda contributed an involved, half-page story written without adult or peer assistance.

Cat Paws

Oene (once) apon a time a monter's (monster) name cat paw's was walking then cat paw's saw Dog pin he was But cat paw was not Afraeder (afraid) But cat paw's was the keller (killer) of Dog's So Cat paw's scrached him Then one nigh (night) cat paw's went to Dog Pin's home and tok (took) a Baby pup and in the moneing (morning) Dog pin saw that one of here (her) pups was gone.

As she had all year, Amanda had plot and problem and cast of characters in mind and out they flowed onto paper; she even tossed in apostrophes for the animals.

Arthur's magazine contribution showed progress in his writing and confidence in his literary work. Arthur gripped the black ballpoint pen and wrote his story in slightly dipping and slanting lines. He occasionally asked a tablemate for spelling help.

Playing

I was plan (playing) my nitndeo (Nintendo) yestday Lastnigth (last night), with my bother in ster (brother and sister) palying to with me I was alway fist (first) playingpt my nitndeo I was pllaying super Marion in buckhunt (back) The Eind.

For much of the school year, Arthur wrote repeated strings of letters in his journals and other writing. He rushed to fill the page with something lest his peers see his writing difficulties and an adult come to help. In the magazine piece, only a few weeks after telling me his fear of repeating first grade, Arthur crowned his year with a determined, involved Nintendo story. And Arthur managed one of his ever so shy smiles in acknowledgment.

In order to promote good classroom relations until the close of the year, John and I continued to emphasize the importance of cooperation and respect. In May, we read books on friends and friendship. In one activity, based on our reading of Arnold Lobel's *Frog and Toad Together*, I asked the children to compose their own "List of Things To Do Today" like Frog. Holding the same long, pink-and-magenta-colored paper on which Amanda wrote her "happy drop" poem, I showed my literature group how to number and write their "things to do" across each line just as Frog did.

Deborah sped to the middle of her day:

my list of things to do today

1. Have lunch
2. make bed
3. have super (supper)
4. Put on my James (jammies)
5. woch who's the base (watch "Who's the Boss")
6. Tern off the tv
7. reda stoere
8. ten off the litt (light)
9. go to sleep
10. wake up in the moning

Warren added people:

My List To Do Today

1. Wake up
2. eat breakfast
3. go to baseball game
4. take a nap
5. say good morning
6. go to chrch
7. go to see buers (boys)
8. see Michele
9. go to see Christ
10. see Charles
11. see Daniel
12. see Jerome
13. see Galen
14. see Nicole
15. see fisheys

Illustrated with her trademark boldly colored girl, this time carrying a balloon stretching to a rainbow and sun, Nicole intertwined school and home:

My list whit to do today

1. go to scoohll
2. go to loch (lunch)
3. play outside
4. go to from and gordin (farm and garden)
5. go to kies clob (kids' club)
6. tees John
7. go to mositc (music)
8. go hom whch t.v.
9. do book lits (booklets from our Writing Workshop)
10. aeite dinn (eat dinner)
11. play whith Foo Foo
12. Hafve birthadays
13. aeite (eat) ice krem
14. play whith my bunny (Foo Foo's offspring)

The children's lists reveal their connection to peers ("See Charles"), their teachers ("See Daniel" and "tees John"), our curriculum and classroom environment ("do booklits" and "play with Foo Foo"), and the larger school community ("go to mositc," "have lunch"). They provide evidence in the children's own words that John and I had promoted a sense of belonging and a sense of community for our students. While we succeeded more with some children than others, some feeling more secure and rooted in our classroom than others, the lists show their personal connections to the social and academic world of our classroom and Mayfield.

In closing our year together, and in looking for indications beyond the standardized tests that we had done a good job, John and I continued to look for clues of the children's involvement with our curriculum and community.

In the middle of May, I worked with the class on a rhyming activity. On the top part of a sheet, children were to draw a line from a word on the left with a rhyming word on the right. On the bottom, students were to write their own rhyming words for three given words.

I helped Arthur, eager for the assistance, successfully complete his sheet. After working at the next center, Arthur returned to me and wanted to do the rhyming sheet again; he seemed to need the extra practice in order to develop fluency and confidence. Arthur wrote his name and worked on the sheet for several minutes without my help. When I called for the children to rotate centers, Arthur handed me the sheet for safekeeping. When he returned after his third center activity, Arthur asked for the sheet and completed it. In an admirable juggling act, Arthur maintained contact with me and the rhyming sheet as he completed his other center activities. I was proud of him; it was another example of his year-long development as a learner and participant in our classroom.

The same morning, Ernesto and Matthew, who were fast friends in spite of language differences, had a hilarious time rhyming words. At my center, the two boys worked together on the sheet, and when it came time to rotate centers, they took the sheet to the next center to finish. I watched Ernesto and Matthew finding rhymes, and laugh with newly discovered bad-boy glee at "blouse" rhyming with "mouse," which only spurred on more laughter about "pantyhose." I doubted either child knew what pantyhose were, but it didn't matter; the fun was in their shared laughter.

Ernesto's feeling of social confidence continued the following week when he became our last Student of the Week. In anticipation of his interview, Ernesto came prepared with an address book from home with his telephone number and address written in. As he sat in our teacher chair, Ernesto pulled out the book and turned to the first page. As if on cue, the first questioner asked for Ernesto's telephone number. Ernesto looked through his book as the children looked on at the novelty, and then shyly whispered to me, "My telephone number is . . . " and I relayed the message to the class and wrote it down on the chart paper beside me.

The next questioner asked where Ernesto lived. Ernesto had difficulty reading all of his address and I helped. In the remainder of the interview, Ernesto revealed his favorite food as pizza, favorite book as *Frog and Toad All Year* (which the class reminded me to underline), and he wanted to be a soccer player "when he grew up."

Like a game show host announcing the season-ending finale, I told the class that since everybody had been Student of the Week, John and I would be the last ones. The children turned to each other and laughed so loud it echoed down the hallway; they couldn't comprehend how John and I could be Student of the Week, the reversal of age and power roles a source of humor as their teachers were going to do a "kid thing."

I was actually nervous for my interview. I sat in the chair as John stood beside me and recorded my interview responses. It looked like a scene outside Willy Wonka's chocolate factory as every child in the class frantically waved their hands for my attention. John and the class reread the completed interview.

My mother's name is Gretl. My father's name is Gerald. My phone number is 485–3271. I live at 1700 Concord. My brothers' names are David, Jeremy, and Andrew. My favorite book is *Where the Wild Things Are*. After school, I like to go to the gym. My birthday is December 11. My favorite food is hamburgers. My favorite stuffed animal is Paddington. I want to be a professor when I'm older. When I go "home" I talk with my parents and eat. I have no children.

My body tracing came next. Regrouping the children around the edge of the rug, I lay down on the butcher paper as John traced my outline with permanent black marker. The children's eyes widened at the sight of their two teachers on the rug.

Next, according to tradition, I was to choose two helpers to color in the tracing. Not wanting to disappoint feelings, I couldn't choose. Just as we asked the class on the first day of school to help solve the lunch code mystery, we asked them for advice on choosing. Among other ideas, one child suggested a lottery like we had for Foo Foo's babies. John said that while this was a good idea, it would take a long time. John finally suggested forming a circle and counting off. It was agreed. The children stood and held hands in a circle and counted by threes. "One, two, three" and the third child sat down. After a few rounds only Galen and Charles stood. The other children scowled and frowned that Galen and Charles had won, but accepted it as fair. Before taking the tracing to the back of the room, John laughingly reminded Galen and Charles "not to draw any Turtles on Daniel."

In the afternoon, John helped the children write letters to me.

Dear Danie
    I am 6 yirs old My buthees (brother's) nam is Jason
Yor Fin (friend)
    Kimberly

Dear Danie
    Do you like cande? I do. I lik it pcus (because) it tas (tastes) good.
    Janet

Dear Daniel,
    I'm 6 years old. My birthday is on April 8. I have a 20 volume insiklapeedeea (encyclopedia) and a big dicsunary. Do you?
    From,
    Joshua

Dear Daniel,
    You looking like a Nol (little) Ket (kid). Then go to Mfd (Mayfield) Solt (School).
    Your fnden,
    Gina

Dear Daniel,
My Birthday is October 22.
Love,
Matthew

Recounting birthdays and siblings and favorite things to do, our students revealed their personal connections to me. And several months after the first day of school, when we told the children they could call us "Mr. Meier and Mr. Sierra" or "Daniel and John," we had become simply "Daniel" and "John." In complementary fashion, by becoming the Student of the Week, John and I showed *our* engagement with our own routine *and* with the children. It was a fun and communal way to close one of the children's most valued and treasured classroom activities.

Continuing to promote positive aspects of our classroom community, John and I created an end-of-the year videotape of the children. I told the class that the video would be used for "little kids" entering first grade, and that they would describe their favorite things about our classroom and impart some advice for the "little ones." I typed a sheet for each child to fill out in preparation for the video.

My name is _____. I am a _____ at _____
School in _____. When I was younger, I thought that one
thing you did in first grade was: _____. Here are some of my
favorite things about first grade: 1. My favorite book is _____.
2. My favorite activity is _____ because _____.
3. My favorite time of day is _____. One hard thing about
first grade has been: _____. Here is some advice about how
to get ready for first grade: _____.

I videotaped each child sitting in the hallway, in the classroom, or on the stairs. Some children elected to read their sheet while others, mostly less experienced readers, preferred to talk to the camera.

Keith sat on a chair wearing his trademark heavy green corduroy jacket. He had dictated the information for the sheet, and then improvised the telling for the camera.

Hi. My name is Keith. I'm in first grade and next year I'm going to be
in second grade. The hard things about first grade are the fighting
and the punching and keeping your, you know . . . [He paused here
and I stopped recording, and letting him regain his thoughts, I started
again] . . . You don't have to dress up unless the girls like you and
everything.

> My favorite free choice is football. There are lots of things that I
> like to play. If you want to stay in school, you should learn how to
> read and go to second grade . . . The hard thing about first grade is
> stop fighting and kicking people. My teacher name is John and Daniel.
> Those are my teachers' names.

Pensive, concentrating, Keith instantly engaged the camera with straight-up
honesty, articulating his connections to our classroom and Mayfield as well as
his year-long difficulties in gaining a sense of place and comfort. With a sense
of maturity beguiling his six years, Keith warned the imaginary audience of
first-graders-to-be about "fighting and the kicking" as the "hard part about
first grade." Keith considered it important to use the adult phrase "stay in
school" and added the conditional "if"—only a first grader, Keith already
sensed the fragile nature of staying in school and making it in the outside world.
Calm and gathering his considerable smarts about him, and given his first-
grade experience with us, Keith was one of the most honest and poignant students on the entire video.

Amanda, in black sweater and hair in long pigtails, flawlessly read her
written text.

> My name is Amanda. I am a first grader at Mayfield School. When I
> was younger, I thought that one thing you did in first grade was
> play 7-Up. Here are some favorite things about first grade: 1. (she
> said "one" for the camera) My favorite book is *Frog and Toad* and
> *The Frog Prince.* 2. My favorite activity is panting (painting) pic-
> tures and water color because it is fun for first graders. and it is
> fun to pant with. 3. My favorite time of day is in the afternoon
> becus we do Form (farm) and graden (garden). One hard thing
> about first grade has been: when we take taks (tests) and when
> the teacher screms (screams). Here is some advice about how to
> get ready for first grade: it is really fun but you have to leasn (listen)
> it will be hard.

Listening to Amanda, I remembered as a child that I too thought 7-Up a "big
kids" game. Amanda's comment helped me realize how bits and pieces of our
schooling histories, as teachers and students and families, float and stay in the
air over time, touching down and reconnecting us in unexpected ways.

I also realized that as her first-grade year closed, Amanda wrote and read
her sheet with confidence and ability that the "taks" (tests) hadn't revealed
weeks earlier. And in acknowledgment of our interactional entanglements over
the year, Amanda matched Keith's honesty by noting the difficulty of achiev-
ing happiness in school "when the teacher screms" and school is "hard."

Although a less accomplished reader than Amanda, Maria was determined to read her sheet. It was her way of showing herself and us, and the hidden audience-to-be, the progress she had made both personally and academically. In a white shirt, white sweater, and now wearing eyeglasses, Maria held the sheet with both hands as she sat on a chair. Determined to do the first-grade thing of reading the sheet, Maria read in fits and starts, all the while bravely carrying on as she half-read, half-talked to the camera.

She read the first line, "My name is Maria," and then said "oops" and covered her mouth with her left hand as she looked at the camera. I stopped recording and let her regroup. She glanced at the page again, but couldn't find her place and said from memory, "You need to do hard work." As she had done in some of her reading conferences over the year, Maria "read" the sheet. It was great improvisation.

Maria continued, "My favorite book is *Brown Bear, Brown Bear*. One hard thing about first grade was doing reading. Here is some advice about how to get ready for first grade—do hard work and do good reading and writing."

Maria paused, put the paper down, and smiled at the camera. With the repeated theme of "hard work" in first grade, Maria's perseverance in reading showed both personal and academic growth in our classroom. Although she showed some of the same tentativeness from the first day of school, when her older sister dropped her off and edged Maria into the room, Maria attempted to read the sheet and showed a determined confidence in herself.

Talkative, and somehow managing to smile the entire time, Edward basked in the attention of the camera.

> My name is Edward. My favorite thing that I like to do in first grade is kick the ball high and go outside and when the bell rings
> . . . and we do another thing and I like to go down to Jeff (his occupational therapist) and sing and go swimming (for physical therapy) and to the library (our trips to the local public library) and (here Edward put up one finger as if to say he had one more thing to say) go play baseball, basketball, and I play with Legos, and feed the fish (points to our tank in the classroom library) and feed Foo Foo (points to the cage by the sink). We have a rabbit named Foo Foo and she had some babies (holds up three fingers). But the babies, the teachers they gave them to kids in our classroom. Bye bye (and a wave).

Edward displayed the lively charisma we had seen all year. Speaking without notes, Edward spoke confidently as he operated from a position of power and ease in facing the camera. Feeling loose, Edward delighted in describing his favorite activities ("play baseball, basketball"), explaining classroom particulars ("We have a rabbit named Foo Foo"), indicating points of interest ("fish"), and recounting important classroom history ("but the babies, the teachers they gave them to kids"). Part class impresario, part class historian, part unofficial class mayor, Edward perfectly closed the children's section of our videotape.

After the children finished, John and Belva and I interviewed and taped each other. I filmed John and Belva describing their favorite things about first grade and offering their advice for doing well, and the tape finished with John filming my comments and suggestions. As John and I spoke to the camera and we recorded each other's comments, the video segments touched back to our initial summer interview and our earliest articulation of our classroom-to-be.

John and I showed the video to the children during the last week of school in mid-June. Over popcorn and punch, the children laughed and giggled at the sight of themselves on the big TV screen. Not really meant for younger children, the video was for our students, a digitized record of their faces and words and thoughts of our year together. The children's themes and insights and favorites—they loved to read and write and do free choice, hated the tests and not getting along with others, and advised children to "listen to the teacher" and "work hard"—showed us their tight grip on basic elements of our classroom, and their determined sense of involvement with themselves, each other, and the still-new world of school.

12

The Last Day–
Reflections on 181 Days

This is me.

by Antonia

The events in our lives happen in a sequence in time, but in their significance to ourselves they find their own order, a timetable not necessarily–perhaps not possibly–chronological. The time as we know it subjectively is often the chronology that stories and novels follow: it is the continuous thread of revelation.

Eudora Welty, *One Writer's Beginnings*

Above the noise of our end-of-the-year party, John and I heard a knock at the door. First a hand appeared round the door's edge, then a foot, then a man cradling two extra-large pizzas. John and I looked at each other and rolled our eyes—Jill, Michael's mother, had just started working at the local Pizza Hut and kindly donated pizzas for our party. At the moment, though, with 20 minutes until the end of the school year, more food was the last thing we needed. But as 27 pairs of eyes spied the pizza man, it was too late. So on came the pizzas.

John turned to the class. Clap-clap-clapclapclap went the rhythm of his hands. Clap-clap-clapclapclap went over 50 small, greasy, and sugary hands. Again John clapped. Again the echo. The room was quiet. Just as on the first day of school in September, when Foo Foo stole the show, the pizzas garnered the children's attention on the last day of school.

"Boys and girls, pay attention," John announced. "Thanks to Jill, Michael's mom, we have two kinds of pizza."

The children cheered.

"One's sausage and the other's pineapple and ham. You need to tell me which one you want, and you can choose only *one* kind. How many want sausage?"

As he had all year, for so many different reasons and in so many different contexts, John surveyed the room and counted the upraised hands.

"Okay, now how many want pineapple and ham?"

Again John counted. John then stuck one stubborn curl behind his ear, as he did when he paused to think, and smiled. The children challenged us right to the end as several children voted for both kinds of pizza.

"Okay, then," John said, changing tactics. "I'll come around and you tell me what you want."

As John played pizza delivery man, adding to the already overflowing paper plates of cupcakes, chicken wings, sticky red juice, grapes, strawberries, cookies, and chips, I organized the children's belongings. As we moved about the room together, as on the first day of school when John and I first greeted our students and families, we complemented each other as we tried to bring a calm and communal end to our year.

Along with a few parents who had volunteered to help, I reached under the tables to check the children's green garbage bags bulging with journals, science logs, books, long-lost jackets and sweaters, and a manila envelope containing report card, standardized test score printout, class placement for next year, and our final parent–teacher newsletter. In character to the end, Joey's and Antonia's bags were ripped, Joshua's and Charles's overflowed onto the floor, and Nicole's and Gina's were neatly organized and closed at the top to prevent spillage.

Everyone eventually got a piece of pizza. Dwight dropped his cupcake in favor of battling a large, sagging slice of pineapple and ham. He quickly discovered that a two-handed shove into his mouth did the trick. Janet and Matthew patiently finished what was already in their hands before attempting the pizza. Joshua and Steven maintained a steady conversation as they ate, Janet and Michael ate in silence, and Warren and Edward shut out the commotion by concentrating on consuming as much food as possible.

The children appeared oblivious to the fact that our year together was about to end. I looked at the wall clock. I had looked at the clock so many times during the year, often reassured that no matter the chaos and lack of calm, the clock would keep ticking. Looking around our classroom, the sights and sounds certainly typified our year—lively, loud, moving with energy, and John and I tired and yet undaunted.

"It's almost time to go," I announced to the class. "Please make sure you have everything in your bag and fold your plate if you want to take your food home with you."

Reenacting the first day of school, John and I repositioned ourselves at the doorway, ready to say good-bye to our students and reverse the direction of their appearance in our school lives.

"Be good, Michele," John said and gave her a hug.

"Have a great summer. I'll miss you," I said.

Michele smiled from behind her garbage bag.

"Have a great summer, you two," Margaret, her mother, said as she helped Michele with the bag.

With a characteristically mature "Have a good summer, Daniel and John," Deborah walked out the door with a flip of her hand along with Sue, her mother.

Joshua wanted no part of a hug; he hadn't wanted one all year, and there was no point starting now.

Matthew just smiled and said "Bye, Dan. Bye, John" in typically soft fashion.

"Thanks," Kathryn, his mother, said. "Matthew's had a great year. And relax over the summer. You guys deserve it."

Eugene gave us one last wrap-around-the-knees hug and grinned from under his curls.

"Have a great summer," Anne, his mother, said. "And maybe we'll see you next year."

Joey lugged his ripped garbage bag with one hand, carefully balancing his treasured plate of food with the other.

John playfully grazed the top of Joey's head. "Keep telling those tall tales and take good care of yourself."

"Be good, Joey," I said, "and have a great summer."

On came Dwight, looking sheepish and in no rush to leave as he dragged his bag along the floor. In an unusual public display, Dwight wanted a hug. John gave him one and a "be good," and then Dwight half-draped an arm over my shoulder. Although it was time to catch his bus, Dwight stood in the doorway, not moving, and holding onto our classroom for another moment. Even with the disappointments of his year with us, it was hard for Dwight to let it all go.

When the bell rang, John called for general boarding.

In those last, too-hectic and rushed moments of the school year, John and I wanted to communicate something personal to our students and send them off on a positive, upbeat note. In doing so, in the important little inter-actions by the doorway, the children remained true to their year-long person-alities and character—Nicole and Maria and Janet shyly tried to slip out the door unnoticed and avoid a hug, Michael and Galen approached us with arms outstretched, Amanda kept saying "okay, okay," as we tried to slow her down for a good-bye, and Charles and Edward exited with as much drama and fan-fare as in their first-day entrance.

The room quieted until only Arthur remained. His older sister and two cousins had joined us for the party, and as we waited for Arthur's mother, John and I awarded the bounty of leftover juice, chips, cookies, and fruit to Arthur and his family members. Arthur relished the attention, strutting around the room with the garbage bag slung over his shoulder like Santa Claus. It was the kind of special, individual attention that *all* our students needed during their year, and now Arthur enjoyed the limelight.

Mrs. Joyner, Arthur's mother, arrived, sweetly bringing us gifts of mugs filled with candies.

"Oohh," Arthur said. "Can I have some?"

John and I laughed and pointed to the mounds of food.

After a final round of hugs and "be goods," Arthur and his entourage left.

"Congratulations. We did it!" I said to John.

"I can't believe it's over," John said.

John offered me a piece of lukewarm pizza in celebration. We sat down together on the small, plastic chairs, munching the pizza and listening to the distant shouts of children enjoying their newfound summer freedom. We then surveyed our classroom. The tabletops made for a still-life scene of half-eaten cupcakes, overturned paper cups, sticky punch, and gnawed pizza crusts. The rest of the room looked more barren. Over the last few days, Belva helped us strip the walls and take down our teacher materials and the children's work. Gone now were the weather graphs and calendar materials from our morning meeting area, the pockets for our library checkout system, the children's cut-out paper hands for "Our Job Chart," the graphs showing "Our Birthdays" and "How We Go Home," the hundreds number chart, the long colorful alphabet, and the year-long collection of children's writings and drawings taped to the cabinets behind our desk. The room looked much as it had back in late August.

I walked to Foo Foo's cage. I unhooked the metal handle and helped Foo Foo out of her cage for a well-deserved end-of-the-year run. John tossed his pizza crust into the trash.

"Come on, Dan, let's take a walk."

John and I stepped out into the sunshine of the hallway. Down the hallway in Emily's room, we hugged and high-fived each other and made plans to go out and celebrate later. At the moment John and I were in no hurry to return and clean up our room, and decided instead on a spontaneous victory lap of the school. Back in August, we had traversed Mayfield's hallways looking for extra tables and desks; now we stopped in on colleagues and exchanged "happy end of the years." It was a good feeling—we had made it through the year and now felt like members of the Mayfield community. As John and I visited our colleagues, we also took a peek at their room arrangements; John and I were considering moving our morning meeting area to the library for more sunlight and a better vantage point of the doorway, removing our teacher's desk to increase space for the children . . . twenty minutes after the close of the school year, John and I were already thinking of next September.

Ten months earlier, John and I had organized the "big things" of our shared first-grade classroom. We parceled out cupboard space, found large group tables hidden in storage areas, scraped off old glue spots with small razors, bought plastic tubs for the children's work tools, placed group signs above the tables, set up the fish tank, found two matching 6′x 9′ pink rugs, organized the calendar activities, cleaned the children's cubbies, and arranged the library books. This is the "doing" or active part of classroom organization and teaching.

John and I also had discussed and shared our teaching visions and philosophies, first-grade curriculum, co-teaching schedule, grouping practices, reading and writing program, integration of other curricular areas, and assessment tools. We decided to use and promote mixed-ability literature groups, journals, social interaction and talk, and opportunities for student choice. This is the "thinking" or planning part of classroom organization.

Then, from the moment Charles strode in on the first day of school, the "doing" and the "thinking" aspects of teaching became less distinct, mixing and blending together. Over the course of our year together, John and I fashioned, reflected upon, tinkered with, and changed what we initially set in place. As our classroom evolved and we confronted more rigorous challenges and interactional difficulties than we ever anticipated, John and I kept working toward a comfortable fit between our goals and the particulars of our teaching and learning situation.

And we learned anew that much of teaching is full of the unplanned and the unpredictable—for all the attempts to make it stand still, teaching is a lively art that grows through constant decision-making, planning, and replanning. Our September beginning resembled a play written only in skeletal form and missing key scenes and details of plot. The 30 participants of our classroom, both audience and players, couldn't predict or forecast what would happen. We had no idea that Keith's year would never quite reach a place of comfort and ease. We had no idea that it would take months to discover that Jerome's grandmother was his primary caretaker. We had no idea that Janet and Eugene and Joshua would quietly and with determination hang onto the energy and liveliness of our classroom. We had no idea that I would find myself helping Edward change his clothes in the bathroom, pulling off and then replacing his hard plastic leg braces, and gaining a new sense of respect and admiration for his daily challenges.

What John and I initially set in motion early in September, we could only partially control and manipulate over the course of the year. As John and I learned anew, in a new personal and professional situation, children have the capacity to outwit and outmaneuver even the best of teacher plans. And so they did. And John and I, reflecting and communicating with each other in our journal and in person, made changes both large and small—we implemented and expanded center activities, changed our co-teaching schedule from whole days to a morning/afternoon split, added more worksheets and "structured" activities, sought outside services for students in extra need—all of which improved life in our classroom. John and I were glad for the changes; they revealed our creativity and power to change and improve our teaching in midstream.

During those long fall months, when John and I worked to achieve a sense of rapport in our teaching partnership and a sense of calm in our classroom, we didn't feel successful and competent. New to Mayfield and the district, unfamiliar with each other and the intricacies of job sharing, John and I muddled our way through daily life in our classroom both as we found it and as it came upon us. And as our classroom community quickly took on a certain tenor and feel, the children and John and I played with, fought against, shook, and sometimes just left it all alone to enjoy in moments of serenity and calm.

Such is the movement of teaching and learning. Sometimes it moves like a caterpillar on a sunny day as when Belva and I took the class on a walking field trip to the movies, and sometimes with a spontaneous energy of words and gestures and numbers and colors as when John taught the calendar activities on the very first day of school. At other times, teaching and learning are best left to the mood of the moment, as Ernesto and Matthew laughed over the rhyming sheet and Deborah played the mouse in "The Great Big Enormous Turnip."

Given such varied forms of movement, varying in origin and speed and direction, perceptions of teaching and learning must move beyond the set length of 181 days. The bell rang in the new school year at 8:45 in September and rang out the year at 2:20 in June. But teaching and learning for children and teachers doesn't recognize artificial limits; education extends beyond the first and the last days of a school year. As John and I learned anew through the particular relationships in our classroom, teaching is basically a human, social enterprise. It is "a continuous thread."

When the last day of school ended, John and I needed an Edward, who played class historian on our videotape, to recap the year and provide a sense of closure and reflection. John and I knew we had made mistakes, both big and small, but also that we had done many things well. Looking back on the school year—as we helped the children create their own class rules, read *Alexander and the Wind-Up Mouse*, write lists of "Things to Do," transferred marbles from one jar to another for good behavior, completed calendar patterns and voted on whether it was "sunny" or "cloudy," shared our family trees, conducted Student of the Week interviews—it's hard to retrace steps and separate out the "academic" from the "social," the "child-centered" from the "teacher-directed," the "developmentally appropriate" from the "structured." Sometimes it was one, sometimes the other, often two or more mixed together, like Deborah and the other girls splattering the easel paints on the first day of school. For rarely in classrooms do paints, initially separate in their jars, remain distinct for long—they quickly drip and move into each other, making new colors and shapes.

Our teaching partnership, rare in schools, helped slow the pace of our teaching and afford a critical look at what worked and didn't work in our classroom. Our co-teaching, and the way John and I approached it, allowed us to increase teacher collegiality and sharing of the daily "stuff" of teaching—Maria's reading at Friday reading conferences, Antonia's new story, Ernesto's boat picture—and all the ups and downs in between. In a classroom where so much happened so fast, our partnership helped us chronicle and think about the little and yet important day-to-day dramas. Too often in schools, the sharing of stories about children and teaching happens by chance around the mailboxes or too formally as an agenda item at staff meetings and in-service days—for John and I, it happened on a more immediate, daily basis and served as an integral part of our teaching.

As in any close human relationship, opportunities for communication led to a kind of shorthand. John's coining of "Monday Madness" became a code term for any bad day. "Jazzed" applied to anything in the classroom going well and exciting us about teaching. And what was written in journal form found its way into our face-to-face conversations, as well as the other way around, making for a two-way nurturing of our teaching partnership.

When John and I moved into our classroom in late August and held a spontaneous show-and-tell of our past teaching work, I wondered if our personal and professional backgrounds were too different and would hinder successful communication and rapport. Over the course of the school year, our differences did surface—John wanted group tables while I favored individual desks; I liked using the occasional worksheet while John disliked them; John wanted more teaching of the traditional parts of a story while I found it too abstract for first graders; I wanted to use more phonics instruction while John thought it only broke language into little bits.

But the very process of talking and negotiating, and learning more about each other through the common experience of teaching the same children, ultimately strengthened us as the teachers we already were and as the teachers we wanted to be. And the chance to let our differences surface, the diverse pair of co-teachers we were, served as another layer of diversity and community in our classroom—just as we wanted to create a viable community out of a diversity of children, John and I wanted to forge a unified partnership between us. And over the year, we went back and forth between the two.

Our year together showed us that learning to teach is an evolving process, and that teaching "well" falls along a continuum of experience and reflection and interest. "Good" teaching is not suddenly arrived at, and although John and I had a history of success behind us, we discovered we had a lot to learn at Mayfield. We also learned that teaching well in one situation does not always transfer to another; my skills in a private school setting in Boston and John's in a bilingual classroom in Arizona didn't all fit our shared classroom at Mayfield. We had to adjust, hold onto what we liked, and add what we needed. The more we saw ourselves as adult learners, learning with and through each other, the more John and I relaxed our perception that we had to control and foresee life in our classroom.

Our efforts, both successful and unsuccessful, to make our teaching partnership and classroom work reveal the elastic and resilient nature of classrooms.

This quality of school life affords "teaching room" to promote a sense of rhythm and stability, foster a viable classroom community from a diversity of students and teachers, and create successful teacher–family relations. It also provides enough room for the unexpected and the unplanned for—Foo Foo to transform from he to she, Ernesto to improve his English, Charles to tell my visiting brother, "Stick with me, kid, and I'll be your worst nightmare," Robert to sign the field trip permission form, Edward's mother to walk to school to tell Edward not to "cut up" in class, and Nicole to reveal the identity of the girl in her journal. It stretched beyond the four walls of Room 201, extending to the pulling up of an imaginary turnip/globe, tall tales of jails and hammerhead spaceships, soft poems about rain, and let-me-tell-you-how-it-is advice to "listen to the teacher" and "you don't have to dress up or anything unless the girls like you and everything."

School reform efforts will change and improve upon the challenges that John and I faced during our year together. Hopefully, the bells will be turned off, six-year-olds won't take standardized tests, teachers will get more support, and teaching will become more like the rich and lively vocation it should be. But school reform will only be truly valuable and long-lasting if it matches the specific contexts and situations of teachers, students, and families in their day-to-day school lives. Changing schools can only go so far, for schooling is a way of life, not a static thing to manipulate and fix. All too dynamic, too human, too slippery, schooling is more like an organism evolving over time.

Teaching and learning in classrooms, as John and I learned in our time together, moves and grows—sprints and walks and crawls and flies—with an energy and reason all its own. And the ever-present goal is to work toward an ease of relation, a sense of synchrony between classroom members. Real and lasting educational change, then, comes from the inside out.

Afterword

John and I stayed on at Mayfield for another year. We wanted to continue the work we started. Deciding on a change of scenery, we packed our things and moved to another classroom down the hallway. With a new group of children, John and I taught first grade again. We started the year with the same morning/afternoon schedule, split the curriculum into math/science and language arts/social studies, and made other changes such as adopting a discipline system and modifying Friday reading conferences.

Some of our students moved on—Keith, Robert, Ernesto, Galen, and Dwight went to other schools and we unfortunately lost touch. Our other students stayed on at Mayfield and went to second grade. John and I would pass our "old children" in the hallways and exchange high fives and smiles, the intensity of the previous year's relationship over, leaving a sweetness of memory and a sense of growing up.

After the second year of our teaching partnership, John decided to return to teaching in a bilingual setting. I remained at Mayfield, job sharing with a new partner before teaching full-time. John and I remain friends and colleagues.

Before our former first-grade students graduated from third grade at Mayfield, I sat down with a dozen of them and asked for their recollections of life in Room 201. We all enjoyed the mini-reunion, and I was relieved and pleased by their mostly positive and fond memories of our year together.

"I remember those little books from writing workshop," Maria said, and with third-grade disdain added, "I hated them because I had to do *all* the writing and *all* the pictures, and it was hardly worth it!"

"And I remember Foo Foo," Steven said. "Janet still has one of Foo Foo's babies. It's really big now."

"I remember Foo Foo, too," Warren said. "I remember the day when she had her babies."

"And I remember being Student of the Week," Edward said. "We got to be in the front of the line for the *whole* week. Then the last two weeks you and John got to be Student of the Week."

"I still have all my work from first grade," Michele said. "I have the *Inch Worm* book we made."

"And I still have the crossword puzzle [word find from our class magazine] with everybody's names," Deborah added.

I attended the children's graduation ceremony a few days later. Dressed in gowns, the children told the audience of families and friends what they wanted to be remembered for.

Charles, still the comic, wanted to be remembered for "being nice to little kids and being funny."

Nicole, now even taller and even more graceful, wanted to be remembered for "being a good and independent student."

Amanda wanted to be remembered for "her love of reading."

Michael, wearing a colorful and sparkly outfit under his graduation gown, gazed at his diploma, transfixed by the document.

Then Edward made a triumphant walk across the stage, grinning all the way as he accepted his certificate and the crowd applauded. Watching our former first-grade students, now older and wiser to the world of school, it seemed like yesterday when Joey played the troll, Amanda rolled on the globe, and I helped Edward put his braces back on. After the ceremony, I congratulated our old students and their families, all of us exclaiming that it "seemed like yesterday when . . ."

About the Author

Daniel Meier currently directs a literacy program for preschoolers and works with beginning and experienced teachers. He holds a doctorate in education, and has written on children's language and literacy learning and teacher education. His work has appeared in such publications as *The New York Times Magazine*, *The Harvard Educational Review*, and *The Horn Book*. He lives in the San Francisco Bay Area.